The History of Conservation
Preserving Our Planet

The Establishment
of the Environmental
Protection Agency

Jeri Freedman

Cavendish
Square

New York

Published in 2018 by Cavendish Square Publishing, LLC
243 5th Avenue, Suite 136, New York, NY 10016

Cataloging-in-Publication Data

Names: Freedman, Jeri.
Title: The establishment of the Environmental Protection Agency / Jeri Freedman.
Description: New York : Cavendish Square, 2018 | Series: The history of conservation:
preserving our planet | Includes bibliographical references and index.
Identifiers: ISBN 9781502631282 (library bound) | ISBN 9781502631299 (ebook)
Subjects: LCSH: United States. Environmental Protection Agency--
Juvenile literature. | Environmental protection--United States--Juvenile
literature. | Environmental disasters--Juvenile literature.
Classification: LCC TD171.F68 2018 | DDC 363.70973--dc23

Editorial Director: David McNamara
Editor: Kristen Susienka
Copy Editor: Rebecca Rohan
Associate Art Director: Amy Greenan
Designer: Lindsey Auten
Production Coordinator: Karol Szymczuk
Photo Research: J8 Media

The photographs in this book are used by permission and through the courtesy of: Cover Marmaduke St. John/
Alamy Stock Photo; p. 4 Steve Dunwell/Photolibrary/Getty Images; p. 7 Jeff Barnard/AP Images; p. 8 Wundervisuals/
Getty Images; p.10 Bettmann/Getty Images; p, 12 Library of Congress/Corbis/Getty Images; p. 18 Nagel Photography/
Shutterstock.com; p. 20 Loomis Dean/The LIFE Picture Collection/Getty Images; p. 28 Ted Spiegel/Corbis/Getty
Images; p. 32 Anchorage Daily News/Tribune News Service/Getty Images; p. 37 William Philpott/AFP/Getty Images; p.
40 Todd Bannor/Alamy Stock Photo; p. 42 Reuters/Newscom; p. 45 Corbac40/Shutterstock.com; p. 48 Romrodphoto/
Shutterstock.com; p. 52 Bruseman/E+/Getty Images; p. 54 Reed Kaestner/Corbis/Getty Images; p. 58 Hfzimages/Getty
Images; p. 61 Photo12/Alamy Stock Photo; p. 65 GIPhotoStock GIPhotoStock/Science Source/Getty Images; p. 69 Doug
Kanter/AFP/Getty Images; p. 71 Mark Wilson/Getty Images; p. 74 Pacific Press/LightRocket/Getty Images; p. 79 Jim
Watson/AFP/Getty Images; p. 82 Kristi Blokhin/Shuterstock.com; p. 84 Ricardo DeAratanha/LA Times/Getty Images;
p. 87 George Frey/Getty Images; p. 91 David Grossman/Alamy Stock Photo; p. 92 Irfan Khan/LA Times/Getty Images.

Printed in the United States of America

TABLE OF CONTENTS

Introduction

Pollution is as old as humankind. Wherever and whenever people have dwelled, they have altered their environment and left behind debris from their activities. Archaeologists excavating Paleolithic settlements dating to between forty thousand and ten thousand years ago frequently find piles of litter from the making of stone tools and garbage pits containing the remains of food and broken tools. As nomadic societies gave way to towns and cities, where people lived generation after generation, their effect on the local environment increased. The ancient Romans are famous for creating **aqueducts** to carry water across vast distances to their cities. What is less well known is that lead pollution from the smelters they used to make their pipes could be found all across Europe. As the population and the cities people lived in grew, so did the pollution they produced, as did its effect on the environment and the people and animals.

The Problem of Pollution

Pollution increased significantly in future generations. During the Industrial Revolution (1760–1840), machines enabled people to manufacture products at a much greater volume and rate than when items had to be made by hand. However, factories had

Opposite: This landfill highlights how much trash people produce.

a much greater ability to produce pollution as well as goods. The nature of pollution changed after World War II (1939–1945) because the new technologies developed during the war resulted in the widespread use of synthetic materials such as plastics, which are made from toxic chemicals, and pesticides, which contain long-lasting poisons. These artificial materials had negative impacts on the health of people and animals, some of which are still evident in places where they have accumulated in the soil. These pollutants increased the rates of cancers, physical birth defects, and other health problems. They have resulted in a reduction of **biodiversity**. Biodiversity is important because the more varieties of plants and animals there are, the greater the chance that some will survive a major change in the environment or climate—whether natural or man-made.

Solving a Problem

By 1970, it was apparent that the problems of pollution had to be addressed and solved. Among these solutions were the need for nonpolluting energy sources to replace those used by manufacturing plants and the growing number of automobiles; ways to control harmful materials being discharged into the air and water by industrial plants; and methods to clean up the existing pollution in the environment and repair damaged **ecosystems**. Addressing pollution and environmental issues was such a large problem that it required government resources. For this reason, the Environmental Protection Agency (EPA) was created that same year.

The EPA is a large and complex organization. As an agency of the US government, it engages in legislative, policymaking, legal, and regulatory activities. The EPA plays an important role in repairing the damage that has been done by past pollution and

The EPA oversees the cleaning up of contaminated land. Here, an EPA project manager discusses plans to clean up this abandoned mine site in Oregon.

in protecting the environment from further damage. Protecting the environment involves several types of activities. First among these are identifying and evaluating activities and materials that are harmful to the environment. Second is finding a way to reduce the output of harmful materials, and to safely contain and dispose of them when they are produced. Third is regulating hazards. The EPA creates regulations that require companies to control the production of toxic chemicals and to dispose of them appropriately. The EPA then enforces these regulations to ensure that companies comply. Finally, the EPA funds researchers and issues reports on threats to the environment. The agency works to influence key decision makers in the government and industry to ensure that companies' activities are carried out in a way that does not damage the environment further.

The activities of the EPA ensure that the environment remains safe for recreational use, such as running.

Services Offered

As part of its mission to ensure that the environment in which Americans live is safe, the EPA oversees the cleanup efforts at hazardous waste sites. In the days before pollution was regulated, companies dumped dangerous and contaminating materials. Now, when it is necessary to locate waste storage or processing facilities, the EPA sees that the locations of such facilities are distributed fairly, so that they are not all located in low-income or minority neighborhoods.

The EPA operates at the federal level. However, it works closely with state environmental protection agencies, providing support and guidance to meet the needs of individual states. It also participates in global efforts to combat pollution, which is important because pollution in one location can travel to farther locations. It is necessary for the agency to coordinate its efforts with environmental agencies from other countries to combat **global warming** and climate change by controlling and reducing pollutants that contribute to the problem. Global warming is not a problem that can be fixed by a single country because it is influenced by activities throughout the world.

The EPA supplies information to the public through a variety of means, including a website and printed material. People can access these materials to learn about dangers they might be exposed to within certain areas and ways to make their homes and neighborhoods safer. On a more technical level, the agency provides scientists and companies with access to databases and environmental modeling software that they can use to enhance their own research and development activities.

Since the EPA's inception, the agency has improved people's lives in many ways, making the environment both healthier and more pleasant. It has saved a vast number of people from suffering the effects of devastating diseases such as cancer, lung problems, and birth defects. In addition to alleviating suffering, these health benefits save the public enormous amounts of money for medical expenses, and the EPA has benefited the economy in many other ways. Recently, the EPA has faced many challenges from individuals who wish to reduce the regulation of businesses. People around the country have held rallies and have encouraged Congress to see that the EPA's integrity is preserved.

The EPA is an agency that has revolutionized the way people live in the twentieth and twenty-first centuries. Its continued efforts are necessary to ensure that the protection it offers the public continues.

1

A Brief History of Pollution and Its Regulations

T he regulation of pollution did not begin in the twenty-first— or even the twentieth—century. Ever since people began to live in cities, they have faced the problem of how to safely get rid of pollution.

The Problem of Pollution

From ancient times to the early twentieth century, improperly-disposed-of waste has led to repeated outbreaks of diseases such as **cholera** and **typhoid**. These illnesses, which have sometimes reached **epidemic** proportions, were the result of germ-laden human waste contaminating the sources of drinking water.

Energy generation has also been a longstanding source of pollution. As early as the eleventh century CE, the increasing size of communities and the switch from burning wood to burning coal led to smoke filling the skies over cities. In fact, the first

Opposite: Nineteenth-century industrial smokestacks in Pittsburgh, Pennsylvania, spew pollutant-laden smoke into the atmosphere.

Workers in nineteenth-century factories, like these adolescent workers at a glassworks factory in 1908, were exposed to pollutants from coal-fired, steam-powered machines.

attempt at regulating air pollution was a law instituted by King Edward I in England in the thirteenth century. It tried to restrict the burning of coal. However, that attempt was a failure.

The problem only grew worse with the advent of the Industrial Revolution. During this time, factories installed steam-powered machines, most of which were run by burning coal. This caused clouds of industrial pollution to accumulate above large cities. The famous London fog of the nineteenth century was largely sulfur-laced industrial pollution from the burning of coal. The pollution was not restricted to London, however. It was found in cities around the world, including the United States, well into the twentieth century. In fact, industrial pollution is still common in major cities in China.

Such pollution injured and killed people. For example, for five days in 1948 in Donora, Pennsylvania, weather conditions trapped toxic emissions from the local zinc-smelting facility close to the ground. Over that time, seven thousand people were hospitalized because of **respiratory** problems, and twenty people died. The incident focused attention on the problem of air pollution in the United States and led to the passing of the Clean Air Act in 1963.

Like air, water is critical for life. However, it wasn't until the mid-nineteenth century that people understood the problems caused by dumping waste in water. Throughout most of human history—well into the nineteenth century—both kitchen waste and chamber pots containing human waste were emptied into the street. From there, the waste washed into the sewers and then into the bodies of water from which people obtained their drinking water. Today, in some developing nations, people still do not have access to uncontaminated drinking water. In such areas, thousands of people die of cholera every year.

Prior to the twentieth century, many factories were built near rivers and streams because the energy they needed came from waterwheels. It was common to discharge the industrial waste from the manufacturing process into those same waterways. Until the 1970s, factory waste, chemicals from industries such as leather tanning, and animal waste from butchering were all dumped into waterways. The water pollution became so bad on the Cuyahoga River in Ohio, where flammable chemicals were discharged, that the river caught fire—several times—from the 1930s to 1969. The first incident, in 1936, occurred when a spark from a blowtorch set fire to debris in the river. The 1969 fire was the **impetus** for the enactment of the Clean Water Act (CWA) in 1972.

Pollution only worsened in the twentieth century. World War II decimated manufacturing facilities in Europe and created a tremendous market for US goods while the Europeans rebuilt. In the United States, more factories were created, and new

Dr. Snow and
Water Pollution

In the mid-1800s, people began to consider a relationship between water contamination and disease. However, it took investigating to completely understand and take action to prevent such pollution in the future.

In 1832 and 1849, serious cholera outbreaks killed more than fourteen thousand people. The Soho district of London was a rundown, congested area without proper facilities for sanitation. It also contained cow barns and slaughterhouses. Because there was no proper sewer system, the London government dumped the waste from people and animals into the River Thames, which contaminated the water it supplied to the residents of the city.

Many people living in the Soho area got their water from a water pump connected to contaminated water sources. Since people were drinking this contaminated water, diseases developed and spread quickly. In 1854, an outbreak of cholera occurred in the vicinity of Broad Street (present-day Broadwick Street), and more than six hundred people died.

Rejecting the dominant theory that diseases like cholera were due to "bad air," a physician named John Snow hypothesized that the cause of the outbreak was contaminated water that spread infection caused by germs. He conducted his own research, tracking water consumption and cholera-related deaths through the area. His investigation proved that unsanitary living conditions and water contamination contributed to epidemics. As a result, authorities in major cities began to take steps to control waste.

technologies were developed. As in the past, industrial waste wound up in the water. Some waste was discharged directly into the water. In other cases, it was buried, but it **leached** into the **groundwater**. Water and air pollution (in the form of **smog**) killed large amounts of wildlife and caused cancer and birth defects in people. Throughout the nineteenth century and most of the twentieth century, smog caused people to become sick with respiratory diseases and cancer, and sometimes die. Another form of pollution was acid rain, which was the result of the gases—sulfur dioxide and nitrogen oxide—emitted from coal-fired power plants. These gases made the rain more acidic by mixing with water, oxygen, and other chemicals in the air to produce acids. Acid rain is corrosive. It kills plants; accumulates in bodies of water, killing the fish and animals that live in them; and damages buildings.

Categories of Pollution

There are two main categories of pollution: point source and nonpoint source. The EPA defines point source pollution as pollution that comes from a single identifiable source, such as a particular pipe or factory smokestack. The most common sources of point source pollution are factories and sewage treatment plants. When industrial plants discharge pollutants into the air through smokestacks, these pollutants can travel a long way. They are then washed out of the atmosphere by precipitation, or simply fall to Earth, landing on any surface they encounter. Lead, mercury, and other dangerous elements then contaminate water and soil. Another cause of point source pollution is water overflowing from a sewer system into a nearby body of water. When a storm causes flooding, it washes pollutants such as pesticides and other chemicals from lawns, driveways, and streets into the sewer system, where it mixes with industrial waste from manufacturing facilities. During severe storms, the sewer system can't handle the volume of water, and it overflows, polluting nearby bodies of water. Livestock farms where large numbers of pigs, cows, or chickens are raised can also cause pollution if the animal waste is not treated.

Nonpoint source pollution doesn't originate from a single location. Rain and melting snow that collect on the ground and then run off directly into streams, rivers, lakes, and the ocean are examples of nonpoint source pollution. The runoff from the precipitation picks up pollutants from the ground, including roads, and carries them into these bodies of water. The pollution endangers ecosystems and affects the attractiveness and safety of waters. It can also have an economic impact by affecting tourist revenue from activities such as boating and industries such as fishing.

Mining operations produce both point and nonpoint source pollution. When mining operations are being carried out, large amounts of rock are dug up by heavy equipment. In some types of mining, such as gold mining, the rock is ground up and chemicals are used to separate, or extract, the ore from the surrounding rock. The water containing these chemicals is then discharged. Since pollution from an active mining operation can be traced to a specific mine, it is a form of point source pollution. Long after mines have ceased to operate, however, pollutants can still leach into the surrounding bodies of water, or be carried there by runoff from precipitation. The pollutants that can seep into the water system from abandoned mines include copper, zinc, and arsenic, among others. When sulfur-containing rock combines with air and water, a chemical reaction takes place that produces sulfuric acid. **Heavy metals** such as copper, lead, and mercury are dissolved by this acidic runoff. When these heavy metals are washed into streams, lakes, or other bodies of water, they contaminate them. If people drink the water from such sources, their bodies absorb the heavy metals, which are toxic, damaging the brain, kidneys, and other organs.

Urban and Rural Pollution

Urban and suburban areas are the greatest contributors to nonpoint source pollution because many surfaces are paved, and the terrain is largely covered with buildings made of hard, nonabsorbent materials like brick and metal. They pose two problems: first, all of the precipitation that hits them runs off their surfaces, and second, pollutants collect on them. This combination means that the pollutants that collect on them are picked up by the precipitation and carried away to bodies of water.

fact!

According to the EPA, 44 percent of assessed miles of streams, 64 percent of lakes, and 30 percent of bay and estuarine areas are not clean enough for fishing and swimming. The most common contaminants they identified were bacteria, mercury, nitrogen, and phosphorus.

Urban environments also frequently contain construction sites. Trash from construction sites, including oils and chemicals, is carried into the water system by runoff. Untreated chemicals used to enhance lawns, such as weed killer and pesticides, are often washed from suburban areas into the water system as well.

A large percentage of nonpoint source pollution in the United States comes from agriculture. According to the Farmland Information Center, there are approximately 900 million acres (364 million hectares) of farmland in the United States. Plowing the land loosens the soil, making it easier for rain to wash it

An accumulation of chemicals that nourish plant nutrients can lead to an overgrowth of algae, as seen here.

away, which increases runoff. The land is typically treated with fertilizers and pesticides, which are washed into bodies of water.

Dangers of Pollution

Pollution affects the environment in many ways that endanger human safety and health. According to the nonprofit environmental organization Pure Earth, pollution adversely affects the health of more than two hundred million people worldwide.

Nutrients

It seems counterintuitive that nutrients are bad for the ecosystem. However, too much of a good thing can be as bad as too little. When nutrients, especially nitrogen and phosphorus, accumulate in high concentrations in a body of water, they can have a negative impact on the plants and animals that live in or near it. Plants use nitrogen and phosphorus to grow, and these elements are primary ingredients in fertilizers. However, too much nitrogen and phosphorus in a body of water can cause plants to grow too much—sometimes to the point where they cover the surface of a body of water. Often, this creates a problem with algae. Algae are tiny plants that are eaten by many water-dwelling organisms. When they grow out of control, they can cover the entire surface of a pond or lake, which blocks the sunlight from penetrating the water. The plants that live on the bottom of such bodies of water need sunlight, just like plants that live on land. Deprived of sunlight, they die and decompose on the bottom of the pond or lake. The bacteria that break down the dead plants use up the oxygen in the water. This makes it hard for fish and other aquatic creatures to survive.

In addition to affecting the aquatic ecosystem, the overgrowth of algae can harm people. Some types of algae produce poisons called **toxins**, which can accumulate in the flesh of the fish and shellfish that eat the algae. If the quantity of algae consumed is small, this has no effect when people eat the seafood. However, when there are very large quantities of algae, the fish and shellfish consume much higher quantities, and the level of toxins is much higher. When people eat the fish and shellfish, they can become ill.

An excess of nutrients can result from fertilizers and livestock waste in the runoff from agriculture, in rural areas, and from lawn fertilizer and pet waste in urban and suburban areas. The burning of coal and oil by power plants and industrial facilities also discharges nitrogen into the atmosphere, which in turn **precipitates** to the ground and is washed into bodies of water by rain and snow.

Pesticides and Chemicals

One common source of pollution is pesticides, which are sprayed to kill insects. These chemicals run off from farms and lawns or precipitate into the water supply after being sprayed.

A crop-dusting plane sprays DDT pesticide over a large expanse of alfalfa fields in California.

Unfortunately, they also poison other organisms they come into contact with, such as fish. Older pesticides like dichloro-diphenyl-trichloroethane (DDT) could build up in the bodies of organisms such as fish that swallowed them. Most modern pesticides do not cause this problem, but the trade-off is that many of today's pesticides are toxic at very small concentrations.

Pesticides aren't the only dangerous chemicals that pollute the water system. Oil and gasoline washed off streets pollute the environment with **hydrocarbons** and metals, and runoff from manufacturing and processing plants introduces **solvents**, paints, acids, corrosives, and other types of toxic chemicals into the water system. Human and animal waste, if not properly treated, introduce bacteria, viruses, and parasites into the water system through runoff, overflowing or faulty sewage systems, and improper disposal of waste from boats. Some of these organisms can cause diseases in people, such as cholera and the Norwalk virus, which cause intestinal illness. Plastics, metals, and other materials discarded as trash can also leach harmful chemicals into the environment and harm plants and animals.

Effects on Biodiversity

Pollution reduces biodiversity. This in turn reduces the chance that a species can survive a change in the climate or environment. The dying-off of a species can affect the survival of species that rely on it for food. Other species may reproduce unchecked because a predator no longer exists, and overpopulation of a species can result in members dying from starvation. In addition, too many members of a species in a given environment can devastate that environment by eating or destroying too much vegetation. If this depletes sources of food needed by other species in the environment, another species may die off.

Because of the widespread damage that can be caused by pollution, governments in the 1960s and 1970s decided that it was necessary to regulate many sources of pollution. This was the major impetus behind the creation of the EPA.

Protecting the Environment

The post–World War II increase in pollution, brought about by expanding urbanization and industrialization, led Senator James E. Murray (D-Montana) to introduce the Resources and Conservation Act in the eighty-sixth Congress in 1960. In the years that followed, during the presidential administrations of John F. Kennedy and Lyndon B. Johnson, the Soil Conservation

Reduction in Sulfur Dioxide in the Air

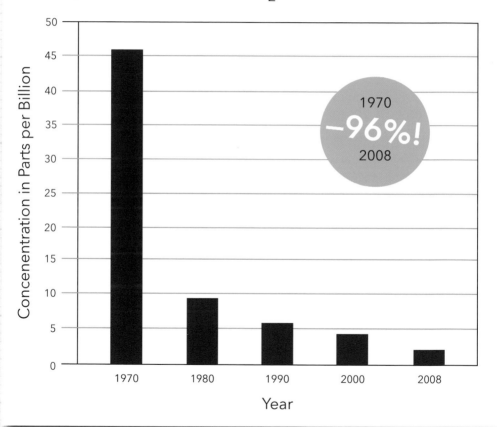

Sulphur Dioxide (SO_2) Trend, 1970–2008

Concenentration in Parts per Billion (y-axis)

Year (x-axis)

1970

−96%!

2008

Since the EPA was founded in the 1970s, the amount of major contaminants such as sulfur dioxide (SO_2) in the air has steadily decreased from decade to decade.

Service (SCS) of the US Department of Agriculture was called upon to address a range of new environmental issues. In 1962, the SCS began the Resource Conservation and Development program (RC&D) in which the SCS worked with landowners to draft long-term economic development plans for large project areas.

Also in 1962, the book *Silent Spring* by Rachel Carson was published. In it, Carson warned the public about the catastrophic effects that the widespread use of pesticides could have on the environment. The book fueled a growing concern with environmental issues in the 1960s and 1970s.

By the late 1960s, Congress recognized the need to address environmental issues in a systematic manner. In 1968, the chairman of the Senate Committee on Interior and Insular Affairs, Senator Henry M. Jackson, and the chairman of the House Committee on Science and Astronautics, George Miller, convened a **colloquium** to devise a national environmental policy and control the actions of federal agencies that were affecting the environment. The result was the National Environmental Policy Act (NEPA), which established the Council on Environmental Quality under the authority of the president. The law required that environmental impact statements be prepared before any federal agency took an action that could affect the environment.

In 1970, President Richard Nixon issued an **executive order** establishing the EPA. The US House of Representatives and Senate **ratified** the order, and on December 2, 1970, the EPA was created. The agency was headed by William Ruckelshaus, an administrator appointed by the president and approved by Congress.

The role of the EPA is to consolidate in one place all federal research, monitoring, standards, and enforcement activities to protect the environment. The goal of the EPA is to provide a clean, healthy environment for the American people. Today, it is headquartered in Washington, DC, and has numerous regional offices and laboratories.

The EPA writes and enforces regulations based on the laws passed by Congress to protect the environment and people's health. To ensure that the regulations are complied with, the EPA has the power to levy fines and impose **sanctions**, among other measures. In addition to regulation, the agency works with industries and governments on voluntary programs designed to conserve energy and prevent pollution. The agency also funds and carries out research.

Early Actions

In 1971, the EPA created national standards for six pollutants that are commonly found in emissions from automobiles and factories. These pollutants have serious negative effects on the environment. Included in the list are sulfur oxides, **particulate** matter, carbon monoxide, photochemical oxidants, and nitrogen oxides. The EPA defined air pollution danger levels for these toxic chemicals. Later the same year, it implemented testing of motor vehicles to determine their fuel efficiency.

The EPA doesn't just create regulations. It also works with representatives of other countries to address issues of importance to both the United States and the rest of the world. For example, in 1972, the United States and Canada agreed to clean up pollution in the Great Lakes, which provide 95 percent of the United States' fresh water. The Great Lakes are the source of drinking water for about twenty-five million people, so removing pollution from them was very important. The United States and Canada worked jointly on the project because the lakes are bordered by both countries.

The EPA went farther afield than North America in creating working relationships with foreign scientists. In 1972, they signed an agreement with the Soviet Union that established the Joint Committee on Cooperation in the Field of Environmental Protection. In addition to attempting to address air and water pollution, the committee researched ways to predict earthquakes and methods for building pipelines in places where the ground was frozen.

In the early 1970s, the most frequently used pesticide was DDT. It was developed in the 1940s and was the first modern pesticide. It was used to combat insects that carried malaria, typhus, and other insect-borne human diseases, and was used in both civilian and military applications. It was very widely used to control insects that ate crops, as well as in home gardens. However, by the 1970s, scientists began to discover the drawbacks of DDT. First, as a result of its widespread use, many insects developed resistance to it. Since only those insects that survived the DDT reproduced, subsequent generations were immune to it. More importantly, DDT was damaging to insects and animals that benefited the environment, such as bees, killing them as well as the pests. It could travel long distances, affecting insects and animals far from the target site. Also, it accumulated in the fatty tissues in human as well as animal bodies, and could cause some cancers, such as liver cancer. Finally, instead of breaking down or **dissipating**, DDT remained present in the environment for a long period. For these reasons, the EPA banned the use of DDT in 1972 and issued regulations requiring the review of pesticides before they were used. Later, the EPA banned two common lawn and garden pesticides, heptachlor and chlordane, because these chemicals caused cancer in mice and rats. Studies "revealed that about 75 percent of dairy and meat products in the United States contained the chemicals and that virtually every person in the US had residue of the chemical in their bodies, including unborn babies."

Congress passed the Federal Water Pollution Control Act, better known as the Clean Water Act, in 1972. It modified and enlarged the Federal Water Pollution Control Act enacted in 1948. Its purpose was to restore America's bodies of water, prevent their pollution, and maintain the integrity of **wetlands**, which are an important ecosystem. The EPA's National Pollutant Discharge Elimination System (NPDES) permit program controls discharges by industrial, municipal, and other facilities. A few months later, Congress enacted the Marine Protection, Research, and Sanctuaries Act, or Ocean Dumping Act, which controls the dumping of chemicals into the ocean. In 1977, the EPA issued national drinking water standards for the first time. All public water suppliers, such as municipalities, were required to test their water at regular intervals and notify their customers if it didn't meet EPA standards.

In 1976, Congress passed the Resource Conservation and Recovery Act, which gave the EPA authority to control hazardous waste from "cradle to grave." The act covered the generation, transportation, treatment, storage, and disposal of material deemed harmful. The Toxic Substances Control Act was enacted by Congress and signed by President Gerald Ford that same year. Its purpose was to control synthetic and organic chemicals in consumer products and the environment. In 1977, President Jimmy Carter continued the drive to protect the environment by signing amendments to the Clean Air Act. According to the EPA, the stronger protections required by the act "spurred the development of scrubber technology, which removes air pollution from coal-fired power plants." The act included construction grants that created thousands of jobs over five years.

Love Canal

In August 1978, residents in Love Canal, a neighborhood in Niagara Falls, New York, were shocked to find that the ground where they lived was contaminated by chemicals leaking from buried containers. The pollution resulted in serious health problems, including cancer and birth defects. President Jimmy Carter declared a state of emergency, and the EPA helped temporarily relocate approximately seven hundred families. In December 1979, the United States sued Hooker Chemical Company for more than $100 million to cover the cost of cleaning up the company's dump sites in Love Canal and other locations in New York.

The Love Canal disaster moved Congress to pass the Comprehensive Environmental Response, Compensation, and Liability Act, better known as the Superfund Act. The act, passed in 1980, authorized the EPA to identify companies that had contaminated sites and force them to clean them up.

2

The Evolution of the EPA

The EPA radically changed the way that industry handled pollution. In the process, it conferred protections on the public, which previously had no defense against the toxins produced by industry.

Preparing for the New Millennium

In 1978, the EPA enacted two important air pollution regulations. The first one controlled exposure to lead in the air. Even small amounts of lead can cause serious damage to the human nervous and circulatory systems. The second regulation phased out the use of fluorocarbon gases, which were used in spray products such as deodorants, insect repellent, and household cleaners. Scientific evidence showed that fluorocarbon gases had an adverse effect on the ozone layer, the layer of gases that forms in the upper atmosphere around Earth. It is called the ozone layer because it contains more ozone (O_3) than other levels of

Opposite: An asbestos removal team removes sprayed-on asbestos from steel beams in an office building.

the atmosphere. Pollution can cause holes to form in this layer, which can have serious negative implications because the ozone layer shields Earth from the sun's dangerous ultraviolet rays.

Since the late 1970s, there has been a 4 percent reduction in ozone in the Earth's atmosphere. In the 2000s, the EPA stepped up efforts to control emissions from car and air pollution. Instead of using the ozone-layer-destroying chemicals, companies were required to switch to safer **propellant** gases or mechanical pumps. It also ordered the phaseout of PCBs, which are chemicals used in many household and industrial products, including paint. PCBs had been shown to cause cancer, and the fact that they persist in the environment represents a long-term danger. Over time, the EPA has banned a variety of other pesticides and chemicals because of their potential to induce cancer and birth defects. Among such pollutants are the pesticide ethylene dibromide (EDB), which was banned in 1983.

In 1982, the EPA began to address the problem of asbestos in buildings. Asbestos is a fibrous material that had been used as insulation in buildings. Old asbestos was shown to crumble and drift into the air. When people breathe asbestos-tainted air into their lungs, it causes cancer. In 1982, the EPA issued a rule requiring all elementary and secondary schools to test for asbestos and consult with the EPA if they found it was present.

In 1995, the EPA launched the Brownfields Program. Its goal was to clean up abandoned sites contaminated with hazardous waste, in order to return them to productive use. Since the program started, more than 450 sites have been cleaned up under the EPA's auspices. In addition, through the Brownfields job training partnerships, the program has led to the creation of over sixty-one thousand jobs.

Toxic Accidents

In addition to regulating polluting activities, the EPA addresses pollution from industrial accidents and oil spills. In 1984, an accident caused the release of 40 tons (36 metric tons) of a lethal chemical gas called methyl isocyanate at a Union Carbide plant in Bhopal, India. The gas killed or injured 170,000 people in the vicinity, and it continued to cause medical problems for years after. In the wake of the accident, the US Congress enacted right-to-know laws, which allow US communities to learn of chemicals stored nearby and participate in emergency planning. To assist people in identifying hazardous chemicals, the EPA launched the Toxics Release Inventory (TRI), a database that contains information reported annually by industry groups and federal facilities. Companies in industries such as chemical and paper manufacturing, mining, and oil and gas drilling and refining are required to file reports that are included in the TRI, if they produce more than 25,000 pounds (11,339 kilograms) or handle more than 10,000 pounds (4,536 kg) of listed toxic chemicals.

Another type of accident that causes pollution is oil spills, which occur when the hull of a tanker is breached (or punctured). The breaching of a tanker's hull can release millions of gallons of oil, contaminating the environment and killing plants and animals. One such oil spill occurred when the *Exxon Valdez* ran aground in Prince William Sound, on the south coast of Alaska, in 1989. The *Exxon Valdez* spilled 11 million gallons (41.6 million liters) of crude oil into the sound, and Exxon was fined one billion dollars. The spill spurred the adoption of the Pollution Prevention Act,

A worker uses low-pressure hot water to clean up an oil-soaked beach after the *Exxon Valdez* oil spill in April 1989.

which was passed in 1990. The act required changes in the way tankers were built, including that they be double-hulled. It also gave states more say in setting spill-prevention standards.

The worst disasters have resulted from accidents at nuclear power plants. On March 28, 1979, the nuclear reactor in Three Mile Island, Pennsylvania, suffered a partial meltdown. It released radioactivity into the atmosphere and the water in an area in which about three hundred thousand people lived. The release was small, but there was a danger that the containment building around the reactor would blow up, causing widespread death from radiation.

In 1986, an explosion did take place at the nuclear reactor at Chernobyl, in what was then the Soviet Union. The disaster occurred during a late-night stress test of the reactor, during which the safety systems were turned off. A combination of design flaws in the reactor and mistakes by the operators arranging the core caused a steam explosion and a subsequent fire that sent plumes of radioactive by-products into the air for approximately nine days. Subsequently, most of the radioactive material fell back to Earth in the western Soviet Union and Europe. The contamination resulted in deaths from cancer and a wide variety of health problems among the people of Ukraine and Belarus for many years after the event.

Even when not causing an accident, nuclear power poses problems for the environment. The core of the energy-producing reactor consists of rods made of radioactive material. After their usefulness has expired, the rods continue to give off dangerous radiation—sometimes for thousands of years. It is difficult to find a storage location for these rods and to ensure that the containers in which they are stored are sufficiently strong to last until the rods are safe. In addition, people do not want such radioactive material being transported through their communities.

The EPA's International Role

As the twenty-first century approached, the EPA became more involved in international cooperation on ecological matters. In March 1991, Iraqi military forces set fire to five hundred oil wells in the neighboring country of Kuwait, sending plumes of black smoke thousands of miles into the air. The EPA headed a team that went into Kuwait to evaluate whether the air pollution was toxic enough to kill people. After the initial assessment, which showed that the pollution might increase respiratory problems of some people but was not life-threatening, the EPA assisted in the installation of monitoring systems to alert the government if the levels of toxins in the atmosphere rose to dangerous levels.

On a brighter front in international relations, in June 1993, then-EPA-director William K. Reilly headed a US delegation that attended the United Nations Conference on Environment and Development—better know as the Earth Summit. The event, held in Rio de Janeiro, Brazil, was an attempt to approach environmental issues while maintaining global economic growth around the world.

With the dawn of the twenty-first century came a period of increasing globalization, with countries working together to improve economic and environmental conditions worldwide. The EPA continued to be active, too. In May 2001, the agency signed a global treaty on Persistent Organic Pollutants (POPs). More than ninety countries signed this agreement. The value of the treaty to the United States is that when POPs are used in other countries, they remain in the soil for very long periods and accumulate in plants that people eat, even though the chemicals are initially used at distant places.

The Twenty-First-Century EPA

In the 2000s, the EPA continued to work to reduce vehicle emissions. In 2004, it implemented the Clean Air Nonroad Diesel Rule. This required the reduction of emission levels from construction, agricultural, and industrial diesel-powered equipment by more than 90 percent. The rule also required the removal of 99 percent of the sulfur in diesel fuel by 2010. The rule resulted in large reductions in pollutants and soot from diesel engines.

The twenty-first century saw increased interest in recovering (recycling) chemicals expelled in industrial processes. The EPA participated in such initiatives. In 2004, it started the Methane to Markets International Partnership (now the Global Methane Initiative). The program's goal was to encourage the development of ways to recover methane cost-effectively. Reducing global

EPA vs. VEPCo

In November 1999, the US Justice Department, on behalf of the EPA, sued a number of coal-fired power companies for failing to install equipment to control the output of dangerous pollutants, including nitric oxide (NO) and sulfur dioxide (SO_2). These by-products, which are produced when coal is burned, cause breathing disorders and heart disease and lead to acid rain and a depletion of the ozone layer.

In 2003, the EPA won its case against one such utility, the Virginia Electric Power Company (VEPCo). VEPCo owned ten power plants that produced 237,000 tons (215,002 metric tons) of emissions annually. VEPco agreed to spend $1.2 billion to reduce its annual emissions over ten years. To do so, they would install equipment to eliminate 60,400 tons (54,793 metric tons) of NO emissions and 176,500 tons (160,118 metric tons) of SO_2 emissions, and convert the coal-burning plant near Washington, DC, to cleaner natural gas instead.

methane emissions improved air quality and helped protect Earth against global warming.

In 2005, President George W. Bush appointed Stephen L. Johnson to be EPA administrator. Johnson, a twenty-seven-year veteran of the agency, was the first scientist to hold the position of administrator. His appointment was indicative of an emphasis in the early twenty-first century on evidence-based scientific research as a means of solving environmental problems.

At one time, authorities assumed that groundwater was free of contamination. However, in 1996, data from the Centers for Disease Control and Prevention revealed that 318 outbreaks of waterborne disease over the preceding two decades could be traced to drinking water systems relying on groundwater for their source. In 2006, the EPA issued the Ground Water Rule, which requires all water systems providing drinking water, including those using groundwater, to be tested on a regular basis for contamination. If contamination is found, the rule requires equipment to be installed to treat the water to protect consumers.

The EPA and BP

On March 23, 2005, an explosion occurred at an oil refinery owned by BP in Texas City, Texas. Fifteen people died in the explosion. The refinery was BP's largest in the United States, covering 1,200 acres (486 ha), and was capable of processing up to 460,000 barrels (19,320,000 gallons or 73,134,156 liters) of crude oil per day. The explosion was caused by the ignition of hydrocarbon vapor and liquid released from a stack. Investigators discovered that operators at the refinery repeatedly failed to follow written standard operating procedures designed to ensure the mechanical integrity of safety equipment. The stack had been in poor condition for at least four years, and alarms were ignored or didn't function at all.

Here is a bird's-eye view of the wreckage after the 2005 explosion at the BP refinery in Texas City.

The disaster was followed a year later by a BP oil spill that released more than 200,000 gallons (757,082 L) of crude oil on the North Slope in Alaska. A second spill, which occurred in August 2006, was contained after leaking about 1,000 gallons (3,785 L) of oil. EPA investigators found that the cause of the leaks was a pipeline in which sediment had built up because BP had failed to clean or inspect the pipeline as required by law. Furthermore, the investigators discovered that the company had been aware of increasing corrosion in the pipeline. The EPA

EPA Wins
Nobel Prize

Although in the 1980s global warming was merely a hypothesis, more than twenty years of scientific research by thousands of investigators has led to widespread agreement among scientists that there is a connection between human activities and global warming. The Nobel Committee believes that climate change is a serious threat that needs to be addressed before it reaches catastrophic proportions. If that were to occur, it could result in some regions becoming difficult for people to survive in. This could lead to massive migrations and wars being fought because of competition for land in areas where it is possible to grow food.

In October 2007, the Nobel Prize Committee awarded the Nobel Peace Prize to former US vice president Al Gore and thirty EPA employees, who constituted the Intergovernmental Panel on Climate Change (IPCC). This award was given "for their efforts to build up and disseminate greater knowledge about man-made climate change, and to lay the foundations for the measures that are needed to counteract such change."

Today, climate change is a leading factor in environmental and international decisions for many countries around the world, thanks in part to the IPCC's influence.

Criminal Enforcement Division was able to make a case against BP Products North America, and the company agreed to pay a $62 million criminal fine and invest $400 million on safety upgrades. The fine was the largest criminal fine ever levied on a company for violating the Clean Air and Water Acts.

Despite the stiffness of the penalty, BP seemed to learn little and show no more commitment to safety than before the decision. On April 20, 2010, a mere three years after the fine was levied, the BP-operated *Deepwater Horizon* oil rig in the Gulf of Mexico exploded, killing eleven workers and contaminating the Gulf with the largest oil spill in American history. The EPA, along with the governments of the affected states and other federal agencies, engaged in the emergency response. The EPA performed environmental data collection and analysis and carried out cleanups. President Barack Obama signed an executive order that established the Gulf Coast Ecosystem Restoration Task Force, to coordinate Gulf restoration programs and projects. The task force, headed by Obama-appointed EPA administrator Lisa P. Jackson, spearheaded efforts to restore the Gulf Coast ecosystems, encourage economic recovery, and address long-term health issues.

The restoration plan, written by Navy Secretary Ray Mabus and supported by President Obama, dedicated a large percentage of the fines obtained from BP to restoring the Gulf. On March 13, 2014, BP signed an agreement with the EPA barring BP from doing business with the federal government for five years.

The EPA and Human Health

The EPA issues regulations that target specific types of toxins that directly affect human health. Lead is one such element. It has long been known that lead is a **neurotoxin**—a poison that damages

Lead paint peeling from the ceilings or moldings of old buildings can be toxic.

nerves. Lead damages the brain. Many houses built before the mid-twentieth century have moldings and window frames painted with lead-based paint that created a bright white color. When small children or pregnant women accidentally **ingest** flakes of lead paint, the lead can cause brain damage in the children and fetuses. According to the EPA, as of 2010, almost one million children had elevated levels of lead in their blood because of exposure to lead in homes. Lead poisoning can lead to lower intelligence, learning disabilities, and behavior issues. Therefore, in 2010, the EPA implemented the National Lead-Safe Renovation Program to Protect Children and Pregnant Women. Under this program, whenever a house built before 1978 is renovated or repaired, the work must be carried out in a way that protects these populations from exposure to lead-based paint on the surfaces being fixed or replaced.

In November 2010, the EPA went on to create a list of 134 chemicals it had identified as having the potential to disrupt the **endocrine system** of people and animals. The endocrine system consists of glands throughout the body, which produce hormones. Hormones are complex molecules that travel through the bloodstream to various parts of the body, where they affect the functioning of organs and also influence behavior. Some of the hormones affected by the chemicals identified by the EPA are those that control growth, reproduction, and **metabolism** (the basic bodily processes that sustain life). According to the EPA, disruption of the endocrine system can result in birth defects and growth abnormalities, infertility, an increased risk of cancer, and damage to the nervous system and immune system. The EPA offers resources to assist in screening for the chemicals that disrupt the endocrine system, including tests for some of the chemicals.

The Fukushima Earthquake

On March 11, 2011, an earthquake struck the coast of Japan, sparking a massive tsunami near the city of Fukushima, the site of several nuclear reactors that provided electric power. The tsunami damaged the nuclear power plants, releasing radiation into the air.

The EPA operates RadNet, a series of sampling stations located around the United States that are used to sample precipitation, drinking water, and milk. In addition, the system contains more than one hundred air monitors to measure radiation. The stations operate twenty-four hours a day, seven days a week, and alert EPA scientists to the slightest change in

Fire trucks spray water on damaged reactors at the Fukushima power plant in March 2011 to keep them from overheating and exploding.

radiation level. If an event causes radiation levels to rise, the EPA can warn the public, and the government can take appropriate action if necessary.

In the wake of the disaster affecting the Fukushima nuclear reactor, the EPA increased the frequency with which they sampled and analyzed radiation with RadNet. Initially, there was an increase in the level of radiation that spread from the damaged reactor. However, it was not at a level that endangered the American public, and by May 3, the levels declined to a point where the EPA returned to its normal sampling schedule. Data on the radiation levels was made available on the EPA's website.

New Rules for the Energy Industry

In December 2011, the EPA issued the Mercury and Air Toxics Standards. These were the first national standards designed to control the output from power plants of toxic elements such as mercury, arsenic, nickel, selenium, and cyanide, all of which are harmful to people. Even though technology had advanced to the point where it was possible to scrub these elements from power plant emissions, until this point there were no requirements to do so. The new standards limited output to the amount emitted by the best-performing sources found.

The EPA must constantly consider what regulations are necessary to keep new processes and industries from endangering people's health. One example is the technology developed in the twenty-first century to extract oil and natural gas from shale rock. Much of this industry in the United States uses a process called "hydraulic fracturing," or "fracking," to obtain oil and gas. In fracking, liquid under high pressure is injected into holes bored in shale rock or fissures in the rock, in order to force open the fissures and obtain the oil or natural gas. In 2012, the EPA issued updated standards for the oil and natural gas industry in regard to fracking.

According to the EPA, as of 2014, more than eleven thousand new hydraulically fractured gas wells were being drilled annually. Fracking releases volatile organic compounds (VOCs) into the atmosphere. VOCs are solid chemical compounds that easily convert to a gaseous form at normal atmospheric pressure. VOCs irritate the eyes, nose, and throat, and can harm the liver, kidneys, and central nervous system. The goal of the new rules is to produce a nearly 95 percent reduction in emissions of VOCs, primarily by capturing natural gas, which escapes into the air. The captured natural gas could then be sold.

Greenhouse Gases, Global Warming, and Climate Change

After a thorough examination of the science and careful consideration of public comments, in December 2009, the EPA formally announced that **greenhouse gases** represented a threat to the health and welfare of the American people. Therefore, the EPA stated that, under the terms of the Clean Air Act, they could regulate greenhouse gases that can lead to climate change.

They established that six greenhouse gases were a danger to the health of the public. The six gases are carbon dioxide (CO_2), methane (CH_4), nitrous oxide (N_2O), hydrofluorocarbons (HFCs), perfluorocarbons (PFCs), and sulfur hexafluoride (SF_6). The EPA also stated that the emissions from motor vehicles were a major source of these gases.

Greenhouse gases play a major role in global warming and climate change. Climate change is a change in the typical weather in a particular region. This change is established by measuring temperature, wind patterns, precipitation, storms, and other elements of weather. "Global climate change" refers to a change in the climate of the entire earth. The earth's climate changes naturally over time. However, current changes in the global climate are occurring at a faster rate and with greater intensity than the gradual change in climate experienced in the past as a result of natural forces.

The term "greenhouse effect" refers to the fact that when these gases collect in the atmosphere, they trap heat from the sun that radiates onto the surface of Earth. They keep the heat from dissipating into space. Thus, the greenhouse gases in the atmosphere act like the panes of glass in a greenhouse. To some extent, the greenhouse effect is beneficial because it keeps Earth in a temperature range that can support life. If

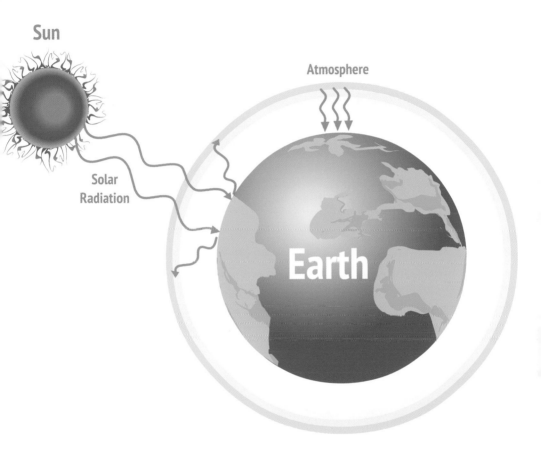

Sun

Atmosphere

Solar
Radiation

Earth

When heat from the sun hits Earth and bounces back into the
atmosphere, greenhouse gases in the atmosphere reflect the
heat back to Earth, resulting in global warming. This is called the
greenhouse effect.

there were no greenhouse gases in the atmosphere, Earth would be too cold to support life. However, over the past two hundred years, human activities that result in the emission of greenhouse gases have caused a greater amount to accumulate in the atmosphere. The gases stay in the atmosphere from decades to centuries. In addition, the clearing of forests and wetlands has reduced the volume of plants covering the planet. Since plants absorb greenhouse gases, this activity has further increased the concentration of greenhouse gases in the atmosphere. This growing concentration of greenhouse gases has the potential to increase the temperature of Earth, which can cause changes such as the melting of the ice on the polar icecaps. Melting this ice can, in turn, raise the height of the oceans, which can cause flooding of coastal cities and destroy coastal habitats. Global warming also contributes to an increase in the severity of weather events such as hurricanes and tornadoes, which have both societal and economic effects.

In 2013, President Obama announced a comprehensive strategy for addressing climate change. The key elements were preparing for the effects of climate change, cutting carbon pollution, and providing technical assistance to other countries. Shortly after assuming the presidency in 2017, Donald Trump attempted to reverse many of President Obama's climate change initiatives. For example, he instructed federal regulators to rewrite key rules designed to curb US carbon emissions, lifted a ban on leasing federal lands for coal mining and oil drilling, and rescinded the requirement that federal officials consider the impact on climate change when making decisions. However, according to NASA, climate change continues to be a problem.

In January 2017, NASA reported Earth's surface temperatures were the warmest since recordkeeping began in 1880. The temperature averaged globally was 1.78 degrees Fahrenheit (0.99 degrees Celsius) warmer than it was in the middle of the twentieth century. Furthermore, 2016 was the third year in a row in which a new record for global average surface temperatures was set. There has been a rise of approximately 2°F (1.1°C) from the late nineteenth century to 2016. According to the NASA report, "Most of the warming occurred in the past 35 years, with 16 of the 17 warmest years on record occurring since 2001." The change, according to NASA, was driven largely by increased carbon dioxide and other human-made emissions in the atmosphere. The EPA remains a key agency monitoring, assessing, and taking actions to reduce activities that contribute to global climate change.

3

Influences
of the EPA

S ince its inception, the EPA has done much both to directly protect Americans and to increase their understanding of the effects that pollution has on the environment and people's health. The information that the EPA has provided to the public has fueled movements to better control the effects of human activities on the environment.

Research

One way in which the EPA has influenced the public is through the research efforts that the agency funds and conducts. These activities provide hard evidence of the effects that pollution has on the environment and move people to act in ways that are beneficial. The EPA engages in research, monitoring, and assessment of the environment. It then shares with the public knowledge of the causes and effects of pollution and the best ways to control it.

Opposite: The EPA regulations protect natural areas, like these wetlands in the Florida Everglades.

One technique used by the EPA is computer modeling. In this approach, a computer simulation of the environment is created. The physical and chemical conditions of the scenario can be varied, and the resulting effect on the environment can be observed. This type of research allows scientists to understand what effects a proposed change or particular type of event would have on the environment, and to prepare for them in advance. Monitoring allows people to observe what is changing—for better or worse—in the environment and address problems more quickly.

Controlling Pollution

Keeping track of changes in the environment and predicting their effects helps stop pollution before it has a chance to harm the environment—and human health. By taking measures to evaluate potential hazards and communicating that information to the public, as well as to scientists, the EPA keeps damage from being done.

One effect of the efforts of the EPA is that industries such as coal mining, power generation, and chemical processing have developed systems that produce less pollution and are healthier for people as well as for the environment. It is unlikely that these industries would have made these changes if the EPA had not made both industry executives and the general public aware of the harm that was being done and the long-term negative effects, and enforced regulations in many cases, forcing industries to make changes. By making the public aware of the dangers of pollution, the EPA inspired many people to demand that industry and the government address environmental issues.

Protecting the Ecosystem

The EPA provides information on ways to control pollution, which can be adopted by groups that want to improve the environment. Its protections for important parts of the ecosystem keep the population healthier. One example is the EPA protection of wetlands. The wetlands act as a filtration system, removing impurities from runoff and preventing them from contaminating water supplies. In 1986, the EPA declared endangered wetlands to be a top priority. The agency created the Office of Wetlands Protection. Its purpose was to research the ecosystem of wetlands and educate property owners on why the wetlands are valuable.

Awareness of the benefits of wetlands has led to the creation of constructed wetlands. In urban and suburban areas, retention ponds have been used to capture runoff and storm water. When the water sits in the retention pond, contaminants settle out of the water, remaining behind when the water runs off. Constructed wetlands are a new twist on water filtration that goes beyond retention ponds. In a constructed wetland, a non-wetland area is made into a wetland and planted with appropriate vegetation; the constructed wetland works like a natural one, slowing down runoff waters and absorbing contaminants. Like a natural wetland, a constructed wetland also functions as a wildlife habitat. The EPA has created handbooks and design manuals for constructed wetlands. It also provides a variety of resources for restoring natural wetlands.

By raising awareness of the problems with runoff pollution, the EPA has encouraged the development of new construction approaches that reduce runoff. For example, using **porous** paving materials in constructing roads and parking lots lets storm water and rain filter through the pavement into the ground, instead of running off and carrying contaminants with it. Collecting the runoff into a reservoir under the pavement allows contaminants to sink out of the water, so that only filtered water returns to the **water table**. This is the area where people's drinking water comes from. Other construction techniques that reduce contamination

This is an example of erosion control, using tree plantings, burlap, and wooden stakes.

from runoff include sediment fences, which are knee-high cloth fences at construction sites that trap construction debris, slow runoff, and filter contaminants out of water. Some construction sites plant grass and lay straw around the site, which also cuts down on runoff and pollution.

Assisting with Disasters

When there is a natural or man-made disaster, the EPA is often called on to evaluate its effect on the environment and the danger to public health. The agency communicates this information to the public, which allows first responders and the general public to take precautionary measures. For example, in August 2005, Hurricane Katrina struck the Gulf Coast of the United States with devastating force. It killed almost two thousand people and affected approximately 90,000 square miles (233,098 square kilometers) of land. In the wake of the hurricane, the EPA participated in recovery efforts by testing the soil where infrastructure was damaged and checking for contamination from toxic waste sites and at damaged oil-refining facilities. It also had to restore the air-quality-monitoring networks that had been destroyed, in order to ensure the safety of recovery workers and returning residents. The EPA issued both broadcast and printed information on air quality and other environmental safety issues.

Auto Fuel Efficiency

The EPA has spearheaded the movement to reduce greenhouse gases produced by motor vehicles. Their efforts have not only contributed to a reduction in the amount of pollution from vehicles, but also increased public awareness of and interest in cars and trucks that have better fuel efficiency and use technologies that are less polluting. In the process, the agency has saved consumers money at the gas pump, as auto manufacturers have continuously increased the number of miles their cars can travel per gallon of gasoline used.

The EPA began testing cars in 1971. This resulted in a competition among automobile manufacturers to produce the best gas mileage and the lowest amount of pollution, as these factors provided fodder for advertising to consumers. On June 4, 1973, the EPA required automobile manufacturers to meet standards set forth in the Clean Air Act. Although the automobile

EPA regulations and information contributed to the development of electric cars, like this one.

manufacturers were granted a delay in implementation of the standard by the courts, they were required to install catalytic converters in cars made from 1975 on. These devices contain a chemical that converts certain emissions to a less harmful form before releasing them into the atmosphere. Catalytic converters, it turned out, also enhanced fuel economy. Initially, the auto manufacturers objected to the standards, complaining that the large cars so typical in America in the 1970s couldn't meet them. According to a fact sheet issued by the Pew Charitable Trusts, called "Driving to 54.5 MPG: The History of Fuel Economy," an executive from Ford Motor Company testified in 1974 before Congress that the standards could "result in a Ford product line consisting … of all sub-Pinto-sized vehicles." Despite these objections, the fuel efficiency requirements were passed and became law.

In the 1970s, the OPEC cartel (a group of Mideast oil-producing nations that controlled most of the oil market) deliberately cut back on the amount of oil produced by member nations, in order to increase the price per barrel. This resulted in a rise of gas prices and fuel shortages, including in the United States. It was during this time that consumers started to embrace the concept of more fuel-efficient cars.

The emphasis on greater fuel economy led auto manufacturers to reduce the weight of cars. As the weight of vehicles goes down, their fuel economy increases proportionately. However, contrary to claims by the automotive manufacturers, large cars are still on the road, and Ford's top seller in the twenty-first century is its enormous F-Series pickup truck. Today, trucks are categorized as light-duty, medium-duty, and heavy-duty. Light-duty trucks are vans and pickup trucks; medium-duty trucks range from very large pickups to small trucks with separate cabs; and heavy-duty trucks are tractor-trailer trucks and similar vehicles. In October 2010, the EPA drafted the first fuel efficiency and tailpipe emission standard for medium- and heavy-duty trucks. The rule was finalized in 2011, covering vehicles produced from 2014 to 2018. Heavy-duty vehicles are the fastest-growing segment within the transportation industry; therefore, their contribution to pollution is significant. The EPA estimated that compliance with the standard would produce $50 billion in fuel-cost savings for vehicle owners and operators, and reduce fuel consumption by 530 million barrels of oil. It would also decrease carbon pollution emissions by 298 million tons (270 million metric tons) over the time vehicles produced from 2014 to 2018 were in operation. In November 2011, the EPA and the National Highway Safety Administration issued a joint proposal to increase fuel efficiency and tailpipe emission standards to an average of 54.5 miles per gallon by 2025. The proposed rule was supported by vehicle manufacturers, labor unions, and environmental activists.

The EPA also approached the question of vehicle-based pollution by instituting regulations that made gasoline cleaner. In the early 1970s, it carried out a study of the effects of lead in air pollution. After the study revealed that lead in air pollution posed a health threat, it began to phase out leaded gasoline in 1973.

fact!

The EPA estimates that having trucks use ultra-low-sulfur diesel fuel will result in a 50 percent reduction in the quantity of air pollution produced by diesel-powered vehicles, or 2.6 million tons (2.3 million metric tons) of nitrogen oxides and more than 100,000 tons (90,718 metric tons) of particulates.

In 2006, the EPA turned its attention to the amount of pollutants emitted by vehicles using diesel fuel. The goal of the EPA regulation is to require oil refiners and fuel importers to start producing a form of ultra-low-sulfur diesel fuel, which contains 97 percent less sulfur than standard diesel fuel.

The problems of air pollution are so significant in some places that they require remedial measures beyond those established by the EPA. For instance, in 2009, the EPA recognized that air pollution in California was a greater problem than elsewhere in the country. It granted California permission to set its own auto-emission standards, which are significantly tougher than those established by the EPA federally.

Protecting People, Animals, and Buildings

Beginning with the banning of the pesticide DDT in 1972 and the dissemination of information about the dangers of chemical pesticides, the EPA has contributed to improvements in people's health. It has also helped save many species of animals that were being killed by the use of persistent pesticides. According to the Aspen Institute, DDT interfered with the ability of many birds to reproduce. Among them were peregrine falcons, ospreys, and brown pelicans. Thanks to the actions of the EPA, the numbers of birds, like the eagle, are increasing. In 2007, the eagle was removed from the Endangered Species List.

Acid rain, in addition to harming ecosystems and reducing the amount of fish, damaged buildings and monuments. The EPA's Acid Rain Program was initiated in 1995 to reduce SO_2 and NO emissions. The program uses a method called "cap and trade." In this system, the EPA caps, or limits, the allowable volume of emissions. Each company can choose to reduce its emissions or, once it has used its allowances, buy more from companies that aren't using theirs. The program has been quite successful. In 2007, total SO_2 emissions were 8.9 million tons (8 million metric tons), which met the program's goal of reducing emission below 9 million tons (8.2 million metric tons) by 2010—three years ahead of schedule. This represents a 43 percent reduction from 1990 levels. The reduction in acid rain has reduced erosion of buildings and monuments and protected aquatic wildlife.

Another program granted power plants and industrial facilities the right to produce a certain amount of pollutants; companies that did not use the allowances could sell them to other facilities. In this way, the EPA was able to control the total amount of pollutants while motivating power plants to reduce their output of such emissions by using alternative methods to produce electricity.

As the public became more aware of the negative effects of acid rain, people started to advocate for the use of safer methods of energy generation. This led to a growth in the alternative energy movement and the use of technologies such as windmills and **photovoltaic panels** to generate electrical power. Today, it is not uncommon to see a wind farm or field of photovoltaic panels at a power-generating plant.

Modern industry relies heavily on chemicals to create a wide range of products, from plastics to food. These products make people's lives more convenient and increase productivity. They have spawned industries that make major contributions to the

Arrays of photovoltaic (solar) panels capture sunlight and convert it into electricity.

US economy. However, chemicals require thorough testing to make sure that they are not used in ways that are harmful to people's health or the environment. In the past, compounds such as pesticides, lead in gasoline, and asbestos harmed many people and animals because their effects were not thoroughly investigated before they were put into use. Since implementing the Toxic Substances Control Act in 1976, the EPA has compiled a list of

fact! ■

According to the Aspen Institute, EPA studies demonstrate that in 2010 cars generated 75 to 90 percent less pollution per mile driven than the cars of the 1970s, because of improvements in vehicle technology and fuel economy.

approximately eighty-four thousand chemicals made in or imported into the United States. The agency has engaged in thousands of required or voluntary information-gathering actions. It has restricted the use of about 10 percent of chemicals that companies have requested permission to use. In addition, it performed reviews that resulted in the withdrawal of more than 1,700 applications for use. The companies withdrew their requests because they expected that the use of the chemical would result in action by the EPA. The EPA also obtained voluntary testing information for more than three hundred chemicals.

In addition to regulating the use of toxic chemicals, the EPA has also created a set of computer models and shared it with manufacturers, to encourage them to develop safer chemicals. For example, the EPA's EPI Suite analyzes the structure of a chemical compound and estimates its physical characteristics, such as vapor pressure and melting point, which affect how it will behave in the environment. The EPA's OncoLogic model evaluates a chemical compound's structure to estimate how likely it is to cause cancer. Using the EPA's models lets manufacturers design safer products.

Fighting Global Warming

The effects of global warming are often depicted in popular media in terms of a doomsday scenario. For example, in the movie *The Day After Tomorrow*, a superstorm devastates New York City. Today, the effects of global warming are becoming apparent, increasing the frequency of major storms, droughts, and wildfires, and endangering animal species in the Arctic and in the oceans. A 2015 report by the Pentagon, "National Security Implications of Climate-Related Risks and a Changing Climate," predicted that global warming would increase the danger to the United States from other countries. The reason for this increase in danger is that global warming is likely to disproportionately affect countries near or south of the equator, including Mideastern and African nations. According to the report, "Global climate change will have wide-ranging implications for US national security interests over the foreseeable future because it will aggravate existing problems—such as poverty, social tensions, environmental degradation, ineffectual leadership, and weak political institutions—that threaten domestic stability in a number of countries." Recurring floods, droughts, and higher temperatures will result in a reduction of land that can be used for farming in countries in the southern hemisphere. In contrast, although the distribution of farmland in the United States will change, there will still be adequate land to grow food. The situation has the potential to make the United States the target of desperate nations and/or resentful terrorists from those nations. The EPA has worked to reduce the emissions of gases that contribute to

In *The Day After Tomorrow*, residents of Manhattan flee from a superstorm engulfing the city because of climate change.

global warming and its public outreach, which has increased public awareness of the problem.

Environmental Justice

In addition to direct action, the EPA is endeavoring to protect people through its policies, and it is playing an important role in the environmental justice movement. Environmental justice requires that all people be treated fairly when decisions are made about implementing and enforcing environmental policies. This means ensuring that some populations are not affected by pollution more than others. For example, placing hazardous waste landfills in areas predominantly inhabited by poor people or minorities is a form of environmental injustice. In 1992, the EPA issued a report confirming that low-income and minority populations experience greater exposure to environmental hazards, including air pollution. A disproportionate number of landfills, incinerators, and other hazardous waste facilities are located in or near low-income and minority communities. Furthermore, highways, railroad tracks, and transportation facilities such as ports and airports are more likely to be located near these neighborhoods. The vehicles add to the pollution in the area, which negatively affects the health of these already stressed populations.

The EPA has developed a strategic plan for environmental justice. Their Environmental Justice (EJ) 2020 Action Agenda covers efforts that will be implemented to advance environmental justice from 2016 to 2020. It addresses environmental and public health issues faced by minority, low-income, and tribal and indigenous populations. As part of the plan, the EPA intends to work with members of the community and local law enforcement. The agency's efforts will include providing guidance and training, as well as performing monitoring and evaluation, to ensure that the distribution of waste treatment and storage facilities does not overburden a given community. The EPA aims to reduce the level of pollution in low-income and minority neighborhoods and improve public health, by enforcing compliance with environmental laws. The agency plans to work with regulators from other government agencies to improve conditions in at least one hundred of the most seriously affected communities. Among the issues specifically being addressed are dealing with lead paint, improving drinking water and air quality, and addressing hazardous waste sites.

By 2020, the EPA expects to integrate environmental justice into all its activities, in an attempt to reduce pollution and improve the environment in the most seriously affected communities. The goal, according to the EPA, is to "help to make our vulnerable, environmentally burdened, and economically disadvantaged communities healthier, cleaner, and more sustainable places in which to live, work, play and learn."

Better Waste Management

From its inception, the EPA has focused on the dangers of indiscriminate disposal of waste. Through its efforts to make industrial management and the public aware of the problems with waste disposal, it encouraged them to engage in two important efforts: (1) producing energy and products in new ways that produce less waste and (2) reusing materials that would otherwise be thrown away. Through its focus on these subjects, the EPA has encouraged a major trend that has grown in importance to many individuals and organizations as decades have passed. Many people today prefer to deal with businesses that behave in a socially responsible way in regard to using recycled or repurposed materials in their products and construction. According to the 2015 Nielson *Global Corporate Sustainability Report*, 66 percent of all consumers and 73 percent of millennials are willing to spend more on a product if it comes from a sustainable source.

Public Awareness Efforts

Not everything the EPA does involves enforcing rules. The agency also provides a variety of information to the general public. It publishes reports and maintains a website containing information on a wide variety of topics. Over time, the efforts of the EPA have significantly raised awareness on a number of important topics. The following are some areas in which the EPA has contributed to public awareness of important health and safety risks.

Reducing Energy Usage

Since 1992, the EPA has reached out to both businesses and consumers directly, through the implementation of the Energy Star program. This is a voluntary program in which manufacturers that produce energy-efficient products are granted a label displaying the Energy Star logo. The first products to be so labeled were computers and monitors. By 1995, the EPA had expanded the program to cover other types of office equipment and residential heating and cooling equipment. In 1996, the EPA partnered with the US Department of Energy to expand the program to cover a wider range of products, including appliances, lighting, and home electronics. The support among the public for protection against global warming has generated an interest in using products that require less energy. Therefore, the Energy Star label has become a marketing tool for manufacturers, which has encouraged the creation of more energy-efficient products. The public interest in sustainable building has made the purchase of Energy Star–labeled products appealing to contractors building new homes and commercial and industrial buildings and plants.

The Energy Star program has partnerships with eighteen thousand private- and public-sector organizations. In addition to being beneficial for the environment, Energy Star–labeled products save consumers money. The Energy Star program

The Energy Star logo on products guarantees consumers that the products are energy efficient.

has fueled the development of technologies such as fluorescent and LED light bulbs, and power management systems for office equipment and electronic devices. According to the Energy Star website, in 2009 "Americans used Energy Star to save nearly $17 billion on utility bills and avoid greenhouse gas emissions equivalent to those from 30 million cars." Australia, Canada, Japan, New Zealand, Taiwan, and the European Union have also adopted Energy Star.

Radon Monitoring

In 1988, the EPA launched the EPA Radon Program. It made homeowners aware of a radioactive, colorless gas called radon, which has a tendency to collect in cellars and crawlspaces. Because it is a gas, it is easily inhaled. Radon is also the second-greatest cause of lung cancer (the first is smoking). The EPA and the Surgeon General's Office estimate that radon is responsible for as many as twenty thousand lung cancer deaths each year. The EPA has worked to encourage homeowners to test for radon and install radon detectors. It provides a booklet called "Citizen's Guide to Radon," which is available both in print and online.

Secondhand Smoke

In the early 1990s, the EPA undertook a study of the effects of secondhand smoke. This is the smoke that enters the air when it is exhaled by smokers or given off by burning tobacco in cigarettes, cigars, and pipes, then inhaled along with air by people nearby. In offices, homes, and other buildings where there are heavy smokers or a number of people smoking at the same time, there can be a high concentration of secondhand smoke in the air.

In 1993, the EPA published *The Respiratory Health Effects of Passive Smoking: Lung Cancer and Other Disorders*. According to this report, three thousand nonsmoking people die of lung cancer annually as a result of breathing secondhand smoke. Secondhand smoke irritates the eyes, nose, throat, and lungs, and reduces lung function. It also causes respiratory problems and affects hundreds of thousands of children annually.

According to a report by the Aspen Institute, "10 Ways the EPA Has Strengthened America," secondhand tobacco smoke contains "more than 4,000 substances, more than 40 of which are known to cause cancer in humans or animals and many of which are strong irritants."

When the EPA classified secondhand smoke as a scientifically established cause of cancer, it provided the anti-smoking movement with ammunition to face down the cigarette industry and achieve bans on smoking in public places. In addition, the information provided by the EPA to the public generated a much broader knowledge of the dangers of secondhand smoke.

Online Resources

The EPA started its first website in 1994. Having an online presence has made it easier for the agency to increase public awareness of important environmental and health issues. The website provides public access to information about the EPA's programs and important environmental and health threats. Helpful booklets and brochures, which can be read online, are also available on the website.

In short, in a little under fifty years, the EPA has changed the way that both industry and individuals view the environment, and increased the public's understanding of the need to protect it, in order to provide safe and healthy places for people to live.

4

Challenges Facing the EPA

A s it approaches its fiftieth anniversary, the EPA is faced with two types of challenges. Some are ecological while others are political.

The Politics of Regulation

Although the EPA has done much to improve the safety and health of Americans, its record is not perfect. At times, political influences have interfered with its mission. For example, after the terrorist attacks on the World Trade Center in New York City on September 11, 2001, the EPA issued a series of statements assuring the people of New York City that the air around the destroyed World Trade Center was safe to breathe. At the time, the EPA did not have adequate scientific evidence to state unequivocally that this was the case, and it ignored conflicting data that had been collected.

Opposite: Here is some of the destruction from the collapse of the first World Trade Center Tower in New York City, on September 11, 2001.

President George W. Bush's national security advisor, Condoleezza Rice, had been charged with reviewing the EPA's press releases and public statements after the 9/11 attack. This fact suggests that the EPA's statements were influenced by the White House's desire to reassure the public, rather than based on an accurate interpretation of the dangers. Unfortunately, it later became apparent that the air was not safe when thousands of rescue workers developed serious, chronic, lung ailments. This is just one example of an attempt to make science conform to political stances, and it emphasizes how important it is for an agency like the EPA to maintain its independence.

In 2017, President Donald Trump put an order in place requiring statements, press releases, and reports by the EPA to be vetted by members of his administration before being released. This raises the unfortunate question of whether the public can rely on statements issued by the EPA when they claim that activities are not harmful to the populace—or whether once again these activities will harm people in the long term.

The Flint Disaster

Problems arise when there is a question as to whether the EPA has the power to force state authorities to follow the agency's recommendations to fix an apparent problem. An example occurred in June 2015 when an EPA ground and drinking water regulator, Miguel del Toral, wrote a report and memo to his superiors at the agency. Del Toral reported that since the city of Flint, Michigan, had begun using the Flint River as the source of its drinking and household water, elevated levels of lead had been found in several Flint homes. By that time, the levels had reached 13,200 parts per billion, which indicated that federal action was needed.

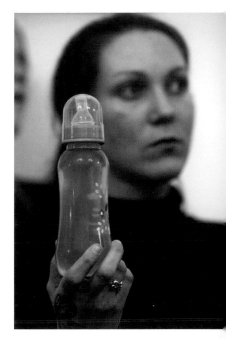

A resident of Flint, Michigan, shows a baby bottle containing contaminated water in 2016.

Del Toral attributed the problem to the Flint government's failure to prevent corrosion in lead pipes that delivered water to the city. Nearly one hundred thousand people live in Flint, and by the time the memo was written, residents had started to experience rashes, hair loss, and other physical symptoms of lead poisoning. In addition, management at the local General Motors factory had found that the water was corroding the engine parts at the plant, so they had found an alternative source of water. Nonetheless, city and state officials continued to reassure the people who lived in Flint that the water was safe.

The EPA has been accused of not releasing the information in Del Toral's report publicly. An EPA administrator claimed the agency could not legally do so because federal law makes the EPA responsible for establishing the standards for states to follow, but doesn't give the agency the authority to force states to meet those standards. According to this administrator, the EPA did try to apply pressure on ever-higher levels of the Michigan Department of Environmental Quality to get them to take action. She stated that the Michigan officials refused to institute corrosion protections that were not required by law.

In January 2016, Michigan governor Rick Snyder declared a state of emergency for the area, leading to the resignation of the head of the Michigan Department of Environmental Quality.

The state put up $28.5 million, and the federal government under President Obama provided another $80 million in emergency funding to fix the problems. The new EPA administrator, Gina McCarthy, pointed out that the failures in Flint demonstrated the need for two mechanisms that do not currently exist in the EPA: a method for the EPA to force state officials to take action when there is an "immediate and substantial" threat to public health, and a clear path for whistleblowers like Del Toral to inform the public about problems that are discovered. The failures in Flint also reveal that politicians who claim that environmental regulations are unnecessary are in denial about the reality of human nature. This leads officials to deny and cover up problems, and the reluctance of cash-strapped cities and states to spend millions of dollars to fix problems. Unfortunately, it is not realistic to expect officials to meet environmental standards without regulations to enforce compliance.

As of the writing of this book, the people of Flint, Michigan, are still recovering; however, there is confidence that the city will have suitable drinking water and updated plumbing. As of March 2017, the state of Michigan agreed to replace any lead or galvanized steel pipes in Flint. This would include eighteen thousand households in the city itself. It is hoped that work on this replacement will be completed by the year 2020.

The EPA Under Siege

The EPA has long been under attack from political conservatives, who are against government regulation. During the Republican presidential campaign of 2016, Donald Trump promised to gut the EPA as part of his plan to remove regulations imposed on corporations. The proposed budget he submitted in 2017 radically cut funding for the EPA. He also issued an executive order requiring the EPA to cut two regulations for every new one they enact.

The EPA's enforcement resources are already severely strained. Cuts could mean a reduction in the agency's ability to enforce the regulations it already has in place. Trying to do more with less increases the chances that the EPA itself will make mistakes. For instance, in 2015, EPA professionals with inadequate technical skills accidentally spilled 3 million gallons (115.6 million L) of toxic wastewater from an abandoned mine into the Animas River in Colorado. One complaint by critics is that, given its current resources and the proposed cuts, the agency can't handle the monitoring, assessment, and **remediation** associated with its current regulations, so it shouldn't be enacting new ones. This is a circular argument. The more its funding is cut, the less it can do, which is exactly the goal of the conservatives who wish to hamstring the agency.

fact!

The EPA's budget has been cut under the last four presidential administrations. With adjustments for inflation, it received an annual average of $10.6 billion under President Bill Clinton, $9.7 billion under President George W. Bush, and $8.8 billion under President Obama. In the June 2017 budget recommendations submitted to Congress, President Donald Trump proposed cutting the agency's funding by $2 billion, or about 25 percent.

It should be noted that even the complete elimination of the EPA would not remove businesses' legal obligation to comply with antipollution laws such as the Clean Air Act and Clean Water Act. These are laws enacted by Congress, and they remain legally binding. The EPA merely creates regulations to define how companies can meet the requirements of these laws and ensures compliance with them. In some cases, the laws state that the EPA

Paris Climate Agreement

Ban Ki-Moon, then-Secretary General of the United Nations, attends a meeting with leaders to mark the enforcement of the Paris Climate Agreement in UN Headquarters in New York City in 2016.

The Paris Climate Agreement is an accord within the United Nations Framework Convention on Climate Change (UNFCCC). It was adopted in December 2015 when 195 UNFCCC members, including the United States, signed it. This was a major step for combating climate change. Only two countries, Nicaragua and Syria, did not sign at the time.

The goal of the Paris Climate Agreement is to keep the temperature of Earth from warming more than 3.6°F (2°C), the level at which rising sea levels, floods, and severe droughts would likely result in serious food shortages in many parts of the world. To do this, all countries must work together.

However, in June 2017, US President Donald Trump announced his intention to withdraw the United States from the Paris Climate Agreement. The official withdrawal process will take four years to complete and have the United States leaving the agreement in 2020.

Reactions from organizations within the United States and abroad varied. However, most reiterated their commitment to combating climate change, regardless of President Trump's decision. Laurence Tubiana, the chief French negotiator of the 2015 Paris Climate Agreement, has stated that countless other countries will honor their climate promises, regardless of the United States' withdraw. French president Emmanuel Marcon, who was highly critical of President Trump's action, posted a video on Twitter, refuting the US president's arguments that complying with the Paris Climate Agreement adversely affects the US economy. Major American companies such as ExxonMobil, Schneider Electric, and Microsoft Corporation have stated they are against the president's action. Bob Iger, CEO of Disney, and Elon Musk, CEO of Tesla, resigned from the president's economic advisory council in response to the president's action. Through these examples, it is clear climate change matters to many people, and the Paris Climate Agreement was close to many people's hearts. It has taken time to recover from the United States' news, but other initiatives sparked around the United States and the world, encouraging others to stand up for the future of the planet.

is to supply permits to industrial plants and manufacturers, and obtaining a permit requires compliance with the law.

The 2017 Republican-run House Energy and Commerce Committee's Subcommittee on Energy and Power held hearings on a proposed "Energy Tax Prevention Act." The act was designed to prevent the EPA from regulating the output of greenhouse gases that contribute to global warming. The act was worded in a way that implied it prevented a tax, although no taxes were actually involved. The Republicans called regulations on greenhouse gases a "tax" on consumers and businesses because they increased the cost of energy. Proponents of this act claimed that the Clean Air Act only gave the EPA authority to regulate industrial pollution such as soot and carbon dioxide, not greenhouse gases like carbon dioxide (CO_2). However, in 2007, the US Supreme Court rendered a decision that the EPA did have the authority—in fact, a legal obligation—to regulate greenhouse gases under the Clean Air Act, if the agency's scientists established that they pose a public danger.

The EPA and Jobs

The EPA is not perfect. However, the agency has done and continues to do an enormous amount of valuable work in protecting public health and safety from dangers in the environment. Many Republicans claim that environmental regulation increases the costs of doing business to the point where it costs Americans jobs. This argument is questionable. First, most businesses, especially those in the power-generating industry, pass their costs along to the consumers who buy their products. In the energy industry, much of the increased cost of regulation has been offset by a major reduction in the cost of oil in the past decade due to the vast new reserves of oil produced by the new oil shale industry in the United States. Second, when a company or power plant has to install or convert equipment to meet EPA standards, the company can subtract a portion of the cost from its corporate income taxes over a certain number of years, reducing the amount it has to pay in taxes and thus regaining much of the money it spent.

The same people who complain that regulation results in a loss of jobs also complain that the need to comply with regulations has required both energy-generating and industrial manufacturing companies to hire large numbers of people to ensure compliance with the regulations! What they actually mean is that regulation has reduced the number of jobs in the coal-mining industry because the air pollution it generates has made burning coal an unpopular way to produce energy. Jim Matheson, National Rural Electric Cooperative Association chief executive, whose group challenged the Clean Power Plan in federal court, has stated that he does not believe that many of the members of his organization will start building new coal-fired plants. Reducing the regulations on coal plants will merely make it easier for owners of existing facilities to keep them operating. New facilities will likely be built to rely on less-polluting forms of fuel.

While coal-mining jobs have declined in recent years, jobs in the fossil fuel industries overall have not. In the past decade, the discovery of how to extract oil from the vast US shale fields in the west has led to an increase in oil drilling and related construction jobs. In addition, as there is more demand for nonpolluting sources of energy, there is a need for more workers who can construct windmills in wind farms and fields of photovoltaic solar panels, which convert sunlight into electricity.

Nor has regulation of the **effluents** and air pollutants produced by manufacturing facilities been the primary cause of the reduction in manufacturing jobs in America. Throughout the late twentieth and twenty-first centuries, large-scale manufacturing plants have

Trumping the EPA

Once he took office in January 2017, President Donald Trump began actively trying to restrict the powers of the EPA. In March 2017, he signed an executive order that directed the EPA to reconsider the Obama administration's Clean Power Plan, which required existing power plants run by electric utilities to achieve a 32 percent reduction in carbon dioxide emissions from 2005 levels by 2050. (Presumably, new power plants that the utilities build will incorporate technology that produces lower emissions than the present ones.) President Obama promoted the rule as a key part of US efforts to fight climate change. In addition, the Obama administration had instituted a **moratorium** on the leasing of federally owned land for coal mining. President Trump's executive order removed the moratorium, allowing the continuation of existing projects and the implementation of new ones. President Trump has also signed a bill that eliminates an Obama administration bill intended to prevent coal miners from polluting waterways by dumping toxic metals such as arsenic and mercury into them. The Republican Party claimed the rule killed coal-mining jobs; however, the Congressional Research Service found that while the rule would reduce certain coal-related employment positions, it would add others, keeping employment numbers steady.

The EPA issued the Clean Water Rule, sometimes called the Waters of the United States rule, in 2015. It allows the

Since taking office, President Trump has signed a number of executive orders. Here, he signs one in January 2017.

EPA to regulate pollution in minor bodies of water, such as streams and ponds. Because a number of legal challenges were filed against the rule in the courts, the Sixth Circuit Court of Appeals put implementation of the rule on hold until the cases were decided. Whether the delay in implementation will hold up depends on the decision of the Supreme Court, which is expected to hear arguments in 2017 as to whether a district court or a federal court of appeals has jurisdiction in hearing the cases. In February 2017, President Trump signed an executive order that required the EPA to rescind or revise the rule.

fact!

switched from hand manufacturing to automated manufacturing using robotics. Some factories are completely automated, to the point where all processing and inspection is done by machine. Manufacturing companies need workers who can operate and maintain automated equipment, not hand-assemble goods. This sort of evolution in jobs is a natural phenomenon, which has taken place throughout history. In the nineteenth century, **cottage workers** producing goods at home or in small workshops were replaced by factories using mechanical equipment. Telephone operators who manually connected phone lines were replaced by electronic switching equipment. Workers in livery stables were replaced by mechanics in garages. Drivers of horse-drawn cabs were replaced by taxi drivers. Now, Uber and Lyft drivers are affecting the taxi industry. The list goes on.

The nature of jobs and industries will continue to evolve as long as there are people. However, if there are going to continue to be people, and those people are going to live safe and healthy lives, it is necessary to protect them from pollutants in the environment and to reduce the number of greenhouse gases in the environment, to the greatest extent possible. If human beings do not control our effect on our environment, nature will do it for us. Eventually, damage to the ozone layer and pollutants in the water, soil, and air will result in increased rates of cancer and other diseases. Global warming will result in more devastating natural disasters and climate changes that cause food shortages in many parts of the world, leading to starvation. It is unlikely that coal will once again become the major fuel used to produce electricity, even if regulations against its use are repealed.

People are very concerned about the environment and its effect on their life and families. There is likely to be a public outcry about industries that pollute, even if there aren't regulations against it, creating a public relations nightmare for those companies. Also, other sources of fuel, such as natural gas, are cheaper to use than coal—and cleaner. For the same reasons, consumers are likely to continue to purchase goods from companies that manufacture products in a "green" fashion; many will continue to boycott companies that pollute or waste natural resources. This trend has been growing throughout the twenty-first century.

If environmental regulations are removed, companies that do not invest in the means to control their pollution will no doubt add to their profit. The additional profit would probably go into the pockets of senior management and stockholders, but would do little for the average worker—who has not had a raise in inflation-adjusted earnings since the 1970s. At least with regulation, the populace has a safer and healthier environment to live and work in. The question we must ask is: Do we want to take control of our effect on the planet? If so, we need the EPA, the United States' leading agency in the fight to ensure a safer and healthier future for America.

UNITED STATES
ENVIRONMENTAL
PROTECTION AGENCY

5

The EPA's Legacy and Future

S ince the 1970s, the EPA has made significant changes in the environment in which American people live and work. It has made the environment cleaner and healthier. In addition, it has educated several generations about the dangers of pollution and, more recently, global warming. In this way, it has changed the public's perspective, making people more conscious of the need to protect the environment in order to protect themselves.

Lasting Contributions to American Health

The efforts of the EPA have successfully reduced air and water pollution steadily over the past several decades. Its work has improved the public's health. Prior to the implementation of the EPA's programs and regulations, horrendous environmental

Opposite: The EPA has protected the people of the United States for over forty years.

This building in California is used to store hazardous waste. EPA regulations ensure such waste is disposed of safely.

conditions existed in many places. These conditions are well documented in historical photos and press accounts. Before President Nixon created the EPA, the country's pollution was increasing, and the state of the environment was declining. Air and water pollution was everywhere. Cities were full of smog. Toxic waste contaminated neighborhoods such as Love Canal.

What would life be like without the work of the EPA? In Los Angeles in the 1950s and 1960s—before the creation of the EPA—the air pollution was so bad that it often stung people's throats when they breathed and brought tears to their eyes. Some days, the smog was so bad that some parents kept their children home from school because they didn't want them to go outside and breathe the air.

To see an example of what uncontrolled pollution looks like in a twenty-first-century urban environment, one has only to look at modern-day Beijing, China, where air pollution is so bad that there are days when it is unsafe to go outside without a face mask. A 2017 article on CNN's website, "Beijing's smog: A tale of two cities," gives some idea of what living without pollution controls in the industrial age is like. The Chinese woman described in the article must pay constant attention to everything she and her family eat, drink, and breathe. She must make sure to buy only organic food and filter her tap water through a special system so it is safe to use for washing, and only bottled water is safe to drink.

EPA regulations don't just make people healthier and longer-lived—they have saved the public and the government trillions of dollars in health-care costs. The results of a **retrospective** review of the effects of the Clean Air Act, carried out in 1997, were noted in a 2017 article by Sean Hecht on Legal-Planet.org, titled "The Trump Administration's False Stories About the Environmental Protection Agency Are Meant to Take the Agency Down." The results showed that had it not been for the regulations implemented by the EPA under the Clean Air Act, "an additional 205,000 Americans would have died prematurely, and millions more would have suffered illnesses ranging from mild respiratory symptoms to heart disease, chronic bronchitis, asthma attacks, and other severe respiratory problems. In addition, the lack of Clean Air Act controls on the use of leaded gasoline would have

fact!

According to a 2016 research study by Nanjing University's School of the Environment, which analyzed over three million deaths in seventy-four cities across China in 2013, as many as 31.8 percent of all recorded deaths could be linked to pollution.

resulted in major increases in child IQ loss and adult hypertension, heart disease, and stroke."

Reducing pollution has affected society in ways that are not always obvious. One aspect of inner-city life—violence—has been positively affected by the EPA's efforts to control air pollution, especially lead. A variety of research supports the fact that the accumulation of lead in the body causes mental changes that can make people more prone to violence. The results of one such study were published as "Association of Prenatal and Childhood Blood Lead Concentrations with Criminal Arrests in Early Adulthood." This study found that in six-year-old children, every 5 micrograms per deciliter of increase in blood-lead levels resulted in an increase of nearly 50 percent in the risk of being arrested for a violent crime as a young adult. According to a 2007 study performed by Jessica Wolpaw Reyes of Amherst College, for the National Bureau of Economic Research, the phasing out of leaded gasoline resulted in about a 56 percent decline in violent crime in the United States. "Childhood lead exposure increases the likelihood of behavioral and cognitive traits such as impulsivity, aggressivity, and low IQ that are strongly associated with criminal behavior."

What the Future Holds

A 2015 report released by the EPA, titled "Climate Change in the United States: Benefits of Global Action," said that climate change could kill twelve thousand people annually in the United States, and that the rising seas that will result from global warming will cause damage to coastal property that will surpass $5 trillion through the year 2100, if greenhouse gas emissions are not reduced. There is still a minority that refuses to accept the evidence, but the majority realizes that the overwhelming weight of scientific research proves that the emissions and waste

In January 2017, vehicles in Lindon, Utah, make their way through thick smog caused by the effects of abnormal temperature changes.

produced by our technology have an effect on our health and that of our planet.

The future of the EPA depends largely on how strongly the American people support the agency and the efforts it puts forth on their behalf. The EPA's programs and regulations have become increasingly important as the impacts of climate change become more apparent. For some time, the EPA has encouraged voluntary efforts to reduce greenhouse gases. Recently, it has begun to make reduction in the output of greenhouse gases mandatory. The EPA's regulations have been challenged in court. However, the Supreme Court has ruled that greenhouse gases are "pollutants," and therefore the EPA has the right—even the obligation—to regulate them.

In 2017, the Trump administration expressed the intention to reduce the EPA's work to control greenhouse gases, along with other agency initiatives. In line with this goal, President Trump appointed Republican Scott Pruitt, the attorney general of the state of Oklahoma, as administrator of the EPA. Pruitt has denied that human activities contribute to climate change, despite the irrefutable scientific evidence supporting that fact. He announced soon after his appointment that he intended to roll back regulations on greenhouse gas emissions and end mandatory reporting of methane and VOC emissions from oil and gas extraction.

In March 2017, Pruitt appeared on a CNBC TV show. During his interview, he stated that he didn't believe that human activities resulted in global warming. His office was subsequently deluged with phone calls from people who were upset by his comments. In April 2017, the official website of the EPA entirely removed information about climate change, sparking new questions, concerns, and frustrations.

President Trump has proposed huge budget cuts to the EPA. The cuts would curtail much of the work of the EPA, including programs that affect environmental safety in the Great Lakes, Chesapeake Bay, and Puget Sound. An April 2017 article in the *New York Times*, titled "What's at Stake in Trump's Proposed E.P.A. Cuts," included the quote: "The cuts are so deep that even Republican lawmakers are expected to push back." Among the cuts likely to face Congressional opposition are: eliminating grants to states to ensure safe drinking water; cuts to the EPA's criminal enforcement program; elimination of environmental cleanup programs; cuts to programs that identify effects of harmful chemicals in products; and the elimination of programs aimed at reducing climate change, including the Energy Star program; among others.

Whether the president will get all the cuts he wants will depend to some extent on people who are concerned about the future of the EPA and the effects of increased pollution on their health. It will be up to the people to insist that their legislators resist attempts to gut the agency.

Scientific research is necessary to discover new threats to the health and welfare of the people. The National Academy of Sciences was established by Abraham Lincoln in 1863, because he felt it was important for the government to have a body that could give it advice based on scientific fact. Scientific results must be accurate and reproducible—which means experiments must measure what they are supposed to, and the same results must be found when an experiment is repeated or done by more than one group of scientists. Since science produces the same result time after time, those who oppose its conclusions and cannot prove them wrong can only resort to forbidding the research. Technology is advancing at the fastest rate in history, and the effects of technology and its by-products on the environment can only be known by studying them.

fact!

Estimates of the amount saved in health and environmental costs by regulations under the Clean Air Act, for the first twenty years it was in effect, range from $6 trillion to $50 trillion, with an average estimate of $22 trillion. The cost to implement those regulations was $523 billion. Thus, the benefits vastly outweighed the costs.

In 2017, many people were concerned about the effects on their health of reducing the power of the EPA. That year, all

Helping the EPA

The EPA has promoted many ideas that have changed the way we think about our relationship with the environment. Here are a few ways the EPA encourages people to get involved in protecting the environment and humanity.

One of the best ways to reduce pollution from runoff is to plant trees, shrubs, or grass in bare areas. The roots of these plants hold the soil together, keeping it from being eroded, and the plants absorb much of the runoff. Use organic fertilizers and nontoxic pesticides. Instead of using pesticide, purchase or attract beneficial insects like ladybugs, which eat garden pests. In addition, some plants naturally repel insects, so planting these among the others can help reduce pests as well. Insect-repelling plants suitable for garden use include flowers (asters, geraniums, nasturtiums, marigolds, and petunias), herbs (mint, catnip, basil, thyme, chives, and rosemary), and vegetables (radishes and onions).

Take the time to properly dispose of household chemicals and items such as batteries that contain toxic material. Do not pour toxic liquids into the water system. Do not throw trash down storm drains. It will travel to the nearest water outlet such as a lake or stream, and can clog the drain, leading to polluting runoff.

Get a group of friends together and do a neighborhood cleanup. Pick up trash and debris or hold a cleanup at a local pond, lake, or stream. Recycle everything you can, including

A group of volunteers participates in a Brooklyn, New York, park cleanup day, improving the local environment.

plastic, glass, metal, and paper. Not only does this reduce the amount of trash in the environment, but it also reduces the energy needed to make more of the material in order to produce products.

Above all, support the EPA and its efforts to keep the environment safe.

An EPA team works at identifying and labeling hazardous waste in California in 2002.

around the country, people held pro-science rallies, demanding that politicians such as Pruitt and Trump make their policies conform to scientific fact, which supported the fact that global warming, climate change, and pollution were real problems.

Proposed cuts to the EPA's budget have also angered many state environmental protection agencies. They feel that the proposed changes move the burden of environmental protection to the states, while cutting funds given to the states.

Most people today don't have to contend with industrial pollution or exposure to lead poisoning because of the regulations of the EPA. However, Americans face the challenge of maintaining a healthy environment and of dealing with new problems as they arise. The future of the EPA, and whether it will have the capabilities to protect the public in the future, depends on the efforts of the people who are protected by its policies and regulations today. The EPA has changed our world significantly since the 1970s, working in many ways to protect people. Now it is up to the people to protect the agency.

Glossary

aqueduct A bridge-like structure containing a channel that carries water from a source, such as a river, to a town or city.

biodiversity The variety of subspecies of plant and animal species in the environment.

cholera An infectious disease that causes fatigue and diarrhea.

colloquium A conference at which experts present information on and discuss a specific topic.

cottage worker A person who makes a product at home or in a small workshop.

dissipate To disperse.

ecosystem A group of plants and animals that interact with a given environment.

effluent Liquid waste that is sent from a factory or treatment plant into a body of water.

endocrine system The system of glands in the human body that secrete chemicals, called hormones, that run the processes in the body.

epidemic Spreading to a very large number of people.

executive order An order that is issued by the president to an agency of the federal government.

global warming An increase in the average temperature of Earth's atmosphere, which may cause climate changes.

greenhouse gases Gases such as carbon dioxide and methane that trap heat radiated from the sun, raising Earth's temperature.

groundwater Water that has seeped deep into the ground, forming the source for springs and wells.

heavy metal A metal such as lead, mercury, or cadmium that is toxic.

hydrocarbons A category of chemicals that contain hydrogen and carbon.

impetus A motivating force.

ingest To draw into the body.

leach To dissolve and sink into the ground.

metabolism The combined processes that take place in the body.

moratorium An authorized delay.

neurotoxin A poison that damages nerves.

particulates Particles in the atmosphere.

photovoltaic panel A type of solar panel that converts sunlight into electricity.

porous Containing pores that allow water and air to pass through.

precipitate To rain or snow.

propellant A compressed gas that forces the contents out of a spray can.

ratify To confirm by voting or issuing authorized approval.

remediation To remedy an environmental problem or to reverse the damage to an environment.

respiratory Related to the lungs.

retrospective Looking back at the past.

sanctions Punishments.

smog A mix of industrial pollution and fog.

solvent A substance that has the ability to dissolve other things.

toxin A poisonous substance.

typhoid An infectious disease caused by bacteria, which produces red spots and severe intestinal irritation.

water table The level at which the ground is saturated with water.

wetlands Marshes, swamps, bayous, and other types of land saturated with water.

Further Information

Books

Carson, Rachel. *Silent Spring*. New York: Houghton Mifflin, 2002.

Christensen, Norm, and Lissa Legge. *The Environment and You*. 2nd ed. Upper Saddle River, NJ: Pearson, 2015.

Harr, Jonathan. *A Civil Action*. New York: Random House, 1996.

Romm, Joseph. *Climate Change: What Everyone Needs to Know*. New York: Oxford University Press, 2015.

Schlottmann, Christopher, Colin Jerolmack, and Anne Rademacher, eds. *Environment and Society*. New York: New York University Press, 2015.

Wimmer, Teresa. *Environmental Protection Agency*. Agents of Government. San Francisco, CA: Chronicle Books, 2016.

Websites

League of Conservation Voters

https://www.lcv.org

This is the official website of the League of Conservation Voters. It discusses the organization's history, current actions, current events, and mission.

Sierra Club

http://www.sierraclub.org

The Sierra Club is the largest nongovernmental organization in the United States and provides news and information on events on its website.

The United Nations Environment Program (UNEP)

http://web.unep.org

The UNEP website provides new and videos on environmental issues and natural disasters around the world.

Organizations

Greenpeace USA
702 H Street, NW, STE 300
Washington, DC 20001

http://www.greenpeace.org/usa

Greenpeace is an international nongovernmental environmental organization working to improve and protect the environment.

US Environmental Protection Agency (EPA)
1200 Pennsylvania Avenue, N.W.
Washington, DC 20460

https://www.epa.gov

The EPA maintains a large amount of information about its activities and services for use by the public.

US Fish and Wildlife Services
1849 C Street NW
Washington, DC 20240-0001

https://www.fws.gov

The Fish and Wildlife Service plays a major role in conservation efforts and is responsible for maintaining the Endangered Species list.

Bibliography

Adora, Andy. "Obama Administration Moves Long-Term Gulf Plan Forward." EPA.gov, September 9, 2010.https://yosemite.epa.gov/opa/admpress.nsf/0/FE2047F24675EADB852577AC006B9905.

Albert, Steve. "Insect Deterrent Plants for the Vegetable Garden." HarvestToTable.com, April 20, 2017. http://www.harvesttotable.com/2009/04/insect-deterrent_plants.

Aspen Institute. "10 Ways the EPA Has Strengthened America." Accessed April 11, 2017. https://assets.aspeninstitute.org/content/uploads/files/content/docs/events/EPA_40_Brochure.pdf.

Berlinger, Joshua, Steve George, and Serenitie Wang. "Beijing's smog: A tale of two cities." CNN, January 26, 2017. http://www.cnn.com/2017/01/15/health/china-beijing-smog-tale-of-two-cities.

Collin, Robert. *The Environmental Protection Agency: Cleaning Up America's Act.* Westport, CT: Greenwood Press, 2006.

Colten, Craig E., and Peter N. Skinner. *The Road to Love Canal: Managing Industrial Waste Before the EPA.* Austin, TX: University of Texas Press, 1996.

Davenport, Coral. "E.P.A. Faces Bigger Tasks, Smaller Budgets and Louder Critics." New York Times, March 18, 2016. https://www.nytimes.com/2016/03/19/us/politics/epa-faces-bigger-tasks-smaller-budgets-and-louder-critics.html.

Davenport, Coral, and Alissa J. Rubin. "Trump Signs Executive Order Unwinding Obama Climate Policies." *New York Times*, March 28, 2017. https://www.nytimes.com/2017/03/28/climate/trump-executive-order-climate-change.html.

Dennis, Brady, and Juliet Eilperin. "Trump signs order at the EPA to dismantle environmental protections." *Washington Post*, March 28, 2017. https://www.washingtonpost.com/national/health-science/trump-signs-order-at-the-epa-to-dismantle-environmental-protections/2017/03/28/3ec30240-13e2-11e7-ada0-1489b735b3a3_story.html?utm_term=.47d57a54c19d.

Ferrara, Adi R. "History." PollutionIssues.com. Accessed March 23, 2017, http://www.pollutionissues.com/Fo-Hi/History.html.

France, Kevin. "EPA Concludes Climate Change Is Biggest Issue of Our Time in Recent Report." Accuweather.com, July 28, 2015. http://www.accuweather.com/en/weather-news/epa-report-climate-change-greenhouse-gas-reduction-kill-12000-people-annually/50680633.

Hecht, Sean. "The Trump Administration's False Stories About the Environmental Protection Agency Are Meant to Take the Agency Down." LegalPlanet.org, March 13, 2017. http://legal-planet. org/2017/03/13/the-trump-administrations-false-stories-about-the-environmental-protection-agency-aim-to-aid-in-destroying-it.

History Channel. "Water and Air Pollution." Accessed March 23, 2017. http://www.history. com/topics/water-and-air-pollution.

Kahn, Chris, "Poll: Unlike Trump, Americans want EPA as strong environmental regulator." Reuters, January 17, 2017. https://www.aol.com/article/ news/2017/01/17/poll-unlike-trump-americans-want-epa-as-strong-environmental-regulator/21656574.

Le, Sarah. "Lead Poisoning a Significant Cause of Inner-City Crime, Say Researchers." *Epoch Times*, August 25, 2016. http://www.theepochtimes. com/n3/2145046-lead-poisoning-a-significant-cause-of-inner-city-crime-say-researchers.

Landrum, Sarah. "Millennials Driving Brands To Practice Socially Responsible Marketing." *Forbes*, March 17, 2017. https://www.forbes. com/sites/sarahlandrum/2017/03/17/ millennials-driving-brands-to-practice-socially-responsible-marketing/#6612b864990b.

Melosi, Martin V. "The Automobile and the Environment in American History." http://www.autolife.umd.umich.edu/Environment/E_Overview/E_Overview4.htm.

NASA. "NASA, NOAA Data Show 2016 Warmest Year on Record Globally." January 18, 2017. https://www.giss.nasa.gov/research/news/20170118.

National Oceanic and Atmospheric Administration. "A Brief History of Pollution." Accessed March 23, 2017. http://oceanservice.noaa.gov/education/kits/pollution/02history.html.

NobelPrize.org. "The Nobel Peace Prize for 2007." Accessed April 8, 2017. http://www.nobelprize.org/nobel_prizes/peace/laureates/2007/press.html.

Pentagon. "National Security Implications of Climate-Related Risks and a Changing Climate." July 23, 2015. http://archive.defense.gov/pubs/150724-congressional-report-on-national-implications-of-climate-change.pdf?source=govdelivery.

Pew Charitable Trusts. "Driving to 54.5 MPG: The History of Fuel Economy." Accessed April 13, 2017. http://www.pewtrusts.org/en/research-and-analysis/fact-sheets/2011/04/20/driving-to-545-mpg-the-history-of-fuel-economy.

Sanburn, Josh. "Why the EPA is Partly to Blame for the
Flint Water Crisis." *Time*, January 22, 2016. http://time.
com/4190643/flint-water-crisis-susan-hedman-epa.

Tabuchi, Hiroko. "What's at Stake in Trump's Proposed
E.P.A. Cuts," *New York Times*, April 10, 2017.

Union of Concerned Scientists. "World Trade Center
Rescue Workers Believed EPA, Ended Up Sick."
Accessed April 16, 2017. http://www.ucsusa.
org/our-work/center-science-and-democracy/
promoting-scientific-integrity/ground-zero-
air-pollution.html#.WPOPOtLyuUl.

US Department of Agriculture National Resource
Conservation Service. "80 Years of Helping People Help
the Land: A Brief History of NCRS." Accessed April
2, 2017. https://www.nrcs.usda.gov/wps/portal/nrcs/
detail/national/about/history/?cid=nrcs143_021392.

US Environmental Protection Agency (EPA).
"BP to Pay Largest Criminal Fine Ever for
Air Violations." October 25, 2007,

US Environmental Protection Agency (EPA). "Controlling
Air Pollution from the Oil and Natural Gas Industry."
Accessed April 9, 2017. https://www.epa.gov/
controlling-air-pollution-oil-and-natural-gas-industry/
actions-and-notices-about-oil-and-natural-gas#info.

US Environmental Protection Agency (EPA). "EJ 2020 Action Agenda." Accessed April 11, 2017. https://www.epa.gov/environmentaljustice/ej-2020-action-agenda-epas-environmental-justice-strategy.

US Environmental Protection Agency (EPA). "Endocrine Disruption." Accessed April 11, 2017. https://www.epa.gov/endocrine-disruption/what-endocrine-disruption.

US Environmental Protection Agency (EPA). "EPA History." Accessed April 2, 2017. https://www.epa.gov/history#timeline.

US Environmental Protection Agency (EPA). "EPA Response to BP Spill in the Gulf of Mexico." Accessed April 9, 2017. https://archive.epa.gov/bpspill/web/html.

US Environmental Protection Agency (EPA). "Japanese Nuclear Emergency: EPA's Radiation Monitoring." Accessed April 11, 2017. https://archive.epa.gov/japan2011/web/html.

US Environmental Protection Agency (EPA). "Region 4: Hurricane Katrina Response." Accessed April 8, 2017, https://archive.epa.gov/region4/katrina/web/html.

US Environmental Protection Agency (EPA). "Responding to Ecoterrorism." Accessed April 7, 2017, https://archive.epa.gov/epa/aboutepa/responding-eco-terrorism.html.

US Environmental Protection Agency (EPA). "Toxic Release Inventory Program." Accessed April 4, 2017, https://www.epa.gov/toxics-release-inventory-tri-program.

US Environmental Protection Agency (EPA). "Virginia Electric and Power Company (VEPCO) Clean Air Act (CAA) Settlement." Accessed April 8, 2017. https://www.epa.gov/enforcement/virginia-electric-and-power-company-vepco-clean-air-act-caa-settlement.

US Environmental Protection Agency (EPA). "Wetlands: Constructed Wetlands." Accessed April 13, 2017. https://www.epa.gov/wetlands/constructed-wetlands.

US Environmental Protection Agency (EPA). "What EPA Is Doing about Climate Change." Accessed June 2, 2017. https://19january2017snapshot.epa.gov/climatechange_.html.

Walsh, Brian. "Politics: The Republican War on the EPA Begins—But Will They Overreach?" *Time*, February 9, 2011. http://science.time.com/2011/02/09/politics-the-republican-war-on-the-epa-begins%E2%80%94but-will-they-overreach.

Index

Page numbers in **boldface** are illustrations. Entries in **boldface** are glossary terms.

About the Author

Jeri Freedman has a bachelor of arts degree from Harvard University. She worked in high-technology companies for fifteen years. She is the author of numerous nonfiction books, including *America Debates: Civil Liberties and Terrorism*, *America Debates: Privacy vs. Security*, *In the News: The US Economic Crisis*, and *When Companies Spy on You: Data Mining and Big Business*.